Pitman Research Notes in Mathematics Series

Main Editors
H. Brezis, Université de Paris
R. G. Douglas, State University of New York at Stony Brook
A. Jeffrey, University of Newcastle-upon-Tyne *(Founding Editor)*

Editorial Board
R. Aris, University of Minnesota
A. Bensoussan, INRIA, France
S. Bloch, University of Chicago
B. Bollobás, University of Cambridge
W. Bürger, Universität Karlsruhe
S. Donaldson, University of Oxford
J. Douglas Jr, University of Chicago
R. J. Elliott, University of Alberta
G. Fichera, Università di Roma
R. P. Gilbert, University of Delaware
R. Glowinski, Université de Paris
K. P. Hadeler, Universität Tübingen
K. Kirchgässner, Universität Stuttgart
B. Lawson, State University of New York at Stony Brook
W. F. Lucas, Claremont Graduate School
R. E. Meyer, University of Wisconsin-Madison
L. E. Payne, Cornell University
G. F. Roach, University of Strathclyde
J. H. Seinfeld, California Institute of Technology
B. Simon, California Institute of Technology
I. N. Stewart, University of Warwick
S. J. Taylor, University of Virginia

Submission of proposals for consideration
Suggestions for publication, in the form of outlines and representative samples, are invited by the Editorial Board for assessment. Intending authors should approach one of the main editors or another member of the Editorial Board, citing the relevant AMS subject classifications. Alternatively, outlines may be sent directly to the publisher's offices. Refereeing is by members of the board and other mathematical authorities in the topic concerned, throughout the world.

Preparation of accepted manuscripts
On acceptance of a proposal, the publisher will supply full instructions for the preparation of manuscripts in a form suitable for direct photo-lithographic reproduction. Specially printed grid sheets are provided and a contribution is offered by the publisher towards the cost of typing. Word processor output, subject to the publisher's approval, is also acceptable.

Illustrations should be prepared by the authors, ready for direct reproduction without further improvement. The use of hand-drawn symbols should be avoided wherever possible, in order to maintain maximum clarity of the text.

The publisher will be pleased to give any guidance necessary during the preparation of a typescript, and will be happy to answer any queries.

Important note
In order to avoid later retyping, intending authors are strongly urged not to begin final preparation of a typescript before receiving the publisher's guidelines and special paper. In this way it is hoped to preserve the uniform appearance of the series.

Longman Scientific & Technical
Longman House
Burnt Mill
Harlow, Essex, UK
(tel (0279) 26721)

W9-AFD-293

Titles in this series

1 Improperly posed boundary value problems
A Carasso and A P Stone

2 Lie algebras generated by finite dimensional ideals
I N Stewart

3 Bifurcation problems in nonlinear elasticity
R W Dickey

4 Partial differential equations in the complex domain
D L Colton

5 Quasilinear hyperbolic systems and waves
A Jeffrey

6 Solution of boundary value problems by the method of integral operators
D L Colton

7 Taylor expansions and catastrophes
T Poston and I N Stewart

8 Function theoretic methods in differential equations
R P Gilbert and R J Weinacht

9 Differential topology with a view to applications
D R J Chillingworth

10 Characteristic classes of foliations
H V Pittie

11 Stochastic integration and generalized martingales
A U Kussmaul

12 Zeta-functions: An introduction to algebraic geometry
A D Thomas

13 Explicit *a priori* inequalities with applications to boundary value problems
V G Sigillito

14 Nonlinear diffusion
W E Fitzgibbon III and H F Walker

15 Unsolved problems concerning lattice points
J Hammer

16 Edge-colourings of graphs
S Fiorini and R J Wilson

17 Nonlinear analysis and mechanics: Heriot-Watt Symposium Volume I
R J Knops

18 Actions of fine abelian groups
C Kosniowski

19 Closed graph theorems and webbed spaces
M De Wilde

20 Singular perturbation techniques applied to integro-differential equations
H Grabmüller

21 Retarded functional differential equations: A global point of view
S E A Mohammed

22 Multiparameter spectral theory in Hilbert space
B D Sleeman

24 Mathematical modelling techniques
R Aris

25 Singular points of smooth mappings
C G Gibson

26 Nonlinear evolution equations solvable by the spectral transform
F Calogero

27 Nonlinear analysis and mechanics: Heriot-Watt Symposium Volume II
R J Knops

28 Constructive functional analysis
D S Bridges

29 Elongational flows: Aspects of the behaviour of model elasticoviscous fluids
C J S Petrie

30 Nonlinear analysis and mechanics: Heriot-Watt Symposium Volume III
R J Knops

31 Fractional calculus and integral transforms of generalized functions
A C McBride

32 Complex manifold techniques in theoretical physics
D E Lerner and P D Sommers

33 Hilbert's third problem: scissors congruence
C-H Sah

34 Graph theory and combinatorics
R J Wilson

35 The Tricomi equation with applications to the theory of plane transonic flow
A R Manwell

36 Abstract differential equations
S D Zaidman

37 Advances in twistor theory
L P Hughston and R S Ward

38 Operator theory and functional analysis
I Erdelyi

39 Nonlinear analysis and mechanics: Heriot-Watt Symposium Volume IV
R J Knops

40 Singular systems of differential equations
S L Campbell

41 N-dimensional crystallography
R L E Schwarzenberger

42 Nonlinear partial differential equations in physical problems
D Graffi

43 Shifts and periodicity for right invertible operators
D Przeworska-Rolewicz

44 Rings with chain conditions
A W Chatters and C R Hajarnavis

45 Moduli, deformations and classifications of compact complex manifolds
D Sundararaman

46 Nonlinear problems of analysis in geometry and mechanics
M Atteia, D Bancel and I Gumowski

47 Algorithmic methods in optimal control
W A Gruver and E Sachs

48 Abstract Cauchy problems and functional differential equations
F Kappel and W Schappacher

49 Sequence spaces
W H Ruckle

50 Recent contributions to nonlinear partial differential equations
H Berestycki and H Brezis

51 Subnormal operators
J B Conway

52 Wave propagation in viscoelastic media
F Mainardi
53 Nonlinear partial differential equations and their applications: Collège de France Seminar. Volume I
H Brezis and J L Lions
54 Geometry of Coxeter groups
H Hiller
55 Cusps of Gauss mappings
T Banchoff, T Gaffney and C McCrory
56 An approach to algebraic K-theory
A J Berrick
57 Convex analysis and optimization
J-P Aubin and R B Vintner
58 Convex analysis with applications in the differentiation of convex functions
J R Giles
59 Weak and variational methods for moving boundary problems
C M Elliott and J R Ockendon
60 Nonlinear partial differential equations and their applications: Collège de France Seminar. Volume II
H Brezis and J L Lions
61 Singular systems of differential equations II
S L Campbell
62 Rates of convergence in the central limit theorem
Peter Hall
63 Solution of differential equations by means of one-parameter groups
J M Hill
64 Hankel operators on Hilbert space
S C Power
65 Schrödinger-type operators with continuous spectra
M S P Eastham and H Kalf
66 Recent applications of generalized inverses
S L Campbell
67 Riesz and Fredholm theory in Banach algebra
B A Barnes, G J Murphy, M R F Smyth and T T West
68 Evolution equations and their applications
F Kappel and W Schappacher
69 Generalized solutions of Hamilton-Jacobi equations
P L Lions
70 Nonlinear partial differential equations and their applications: Collège de France Seminar. Volume III
H Brezis and J L Lions
71 Spectral theory and wave operators for the Schrödinger equation
A M Berthier
72 Approximation of Hilbert space operators I
D A Herrero
73 Vector valued Nevanlinna Theory
H J W Ziegler
74 Instability, nonexistence and weighted energy methods in fluid dynamics and related theories
B Straughan
75 Local bifurcation and symmetry
A Vanderbauwhede
76 Clifford analysis
F Brackx, R Delanghe and F Sommen
77 Nonlinear equivalence, reduction of PDEs to ODEs and fast convergent numerical methods
E E Rosinger
78 Free boundary problems, theory and applications. Volume I
A Fasano and M Primicerio
79 Free boundary problems, theory and applications. Volume II
A Fasano and M Primicerio
80 Symplectic geometry
A Crumeyrolle and J Grifone
81 An algorithmic analysis of a communication model with retransmission of flawed messages
D M Lucantoni
82 Geometric games and their applications
W H Ruckle
83 Additive groups of rings
S Feigelstock
84 Nonlinear partial differential equations and their applications: Collège de France Seminar. Volume IV
H Brezis and J L Lions
85 Multiplicative functionals on topological algebras
T Husain
86 Hamilton-Jacobi equations in Hilbert spaces
V Barbu and G Da Prato
87 Harmonic maps with symmetry, harmonic morphisms and deformations of metrics
P Baird
88 Similarity solutions of nonlinear partial differential equations
L Dresner
89 Contributions to nonlinear partial differential equations
C Bardos, A Damlamian, J I Díaz and J Hernández
90 Banach and Hilbert spaces of vector-valued functions
J Burbea and P Masani
91 Control and observation of neutral systems
D Salamon
92 Banach bundles, Banach modules and automorphisms of C*-algebras
M J Dupré and R M Gillette
93 Nonlinear partial differential equations and their applications: Collège de France Seminar. Volume V
H Brezis and J L Lions
94 Computer algebra in applied mathematics: an introduction to MACSYMA
R H Rand
95 Advances in nonlinear waves. Volume I
L Debnath
96 FC-groups
M J Tomkinson
97 Topics in relaxation and ellipsoidal methods
M Akgül
98 Analogue of the group algebra for topological semigroups
H Dzinotyiweyi
99 Stochastic functional differential equations
S E A Mohammed

100 Optimal control of variational inequalities
V Barbu
101 Partial differential equations and dynamical systems
W E Fitzgibbon III
102 Approximation of Hilbert space operators. Volume II
C Apostol, L A Fialkow, D A Herrero and D Voiculescu
103 Nondiscrete induction and iterative processes
V Ptak and F-A Potra
104 Analytic functions – growth aspects
O P Juneja and G P Kapoor
105 Theory of Tikhonov regularization for Fredholm equations of the first kind
C W Groetsch
106 Nonlinear partial differential equations and free boundaries. Volume I
J I Díaz
107 Tight and taut immersions of manifolds
T E Cecil and P J Ryan
108 A layering method for viscous, incompressible L_p flows occupying R^n
A Douglis and E B Fabes
109 Nonlinear partial differential equations and their applications: Collège de France Seminar. Volume VI
H Brezis and J L Lions
110 Finite generalized quadrangles
S E Payne and J A Thas
111 Advances in nonlinear waves. Volume II
L Debnath
112 Topics in several complex variables
E Ramírez de Arellano and D Sundararaman
113 Differential equations, flow invariance and applications
N H Pavel
114 Geometrical combinatorics
F C Holroyd and R J Wilson
115 Generators of strongly continuous semigroups
J A van Casteren
116 Growth of algebras and Gelfand–Kirillov dimension
G R Krause and T H Lenagan
117 Theory of bases and cones
P K Kamthan and M Gupta
118 Linear groups and permutations
A R Camina and E A Whelan
119 General Wiener–Hopf factorization methods
F-O Speck
120 Free boundary problems: applications and theory, Volume III
A Bossavit, A Damlamian and M Fremond
121 Free boundary problems: applications and theory, Volume IV
A Bossavit, A Damlamian and M Fremond
122 Nonlinear partial differential equations and their applications: Collège de France Seminar. Volume VII
H Brezis and J L Lions
123 Geometric methods in operator algebras
H Araki and E G Effros
124 Infinite dimensional analysis–stochastic processes
S Albeverio
125 Ennio de Giorgi Colloquium
P Krée
126 Almost-periodic functions in abstract spaces
S Zaidman
127 Nonlinear variational problems
A Marino, L Modica, S Spagnolo and M Degiovanni
128 Second-order systems of partial differential equations in the plane
L K Hua, W Lin and C-Q Wu
129 Asymptotics of high-order ordinary differential equations
R B Paris and A D Wood
130 Stochastic differential equations
R Wu
131 Differential geometry
L A Cordero
132 Nonlinear differential equations
J K Hale and P Martinez-Amores
133 Approximation theory and applications
S P Singh
134 Near-rings and their links with groups
J D P Meldrum
135 Estimating eigenvalues with *a posteriori/a priori* inequalities
J R Kuttler and V G Sigillito
136 Regular semigroups as extensions
F J Pastijn and M Petrich
137 Representations of rank one Lie groups
D H Collingwood
138 Fractional calculus
G F Roach and A C McBride
139 Hamilton's principle in continuum mechanics
A Bedford
140 Numerical analysis
D F Griffiths and G A Watson
141 Semigroups, theory and applications. Volume I
H Brezis, M G Crandall and F Kappel
142 Distribution theorems of L-functions
D Joyner
143 Recent developments in structured continua
D De Kee and P Kaloni
144 Functional analysis and two-point differential operators
J Locker
145 Numerical methods for partial differential equations
S I Hariharan and T H Moulden
146 Completely bounded maps and dilations
V I Paulsen
147 Harmonic analysis on the Heisenberg nilpotent Lie group
W Schempp
148 Contributions to modern calculus of variations
L Cesari
149 Nonlinear parabolic equations: qualitative properties of solutions
L Boccardo and A Tesei
150 From local times to global geometry, control and physics
K D Elworthy

151 A stochastic maximum principle for optimal control of diffusions
U G Haussmann
152 Semigroups, theory and applications. Volume II
H Brezis, M G Crandall and F Kappel
153 A general theory of integration in function spaces
P Muldowney
154 Oakland Conference on partial differential equations and applied mathematics
L R Bragg and J W Dettman
155 Contributions to nonlinear partial differential equations. Volume II
J I Díaz and P L Lions
156 Semigroups of linear operators: an introduction
A C McBride
157 Ordinary and partial differential equations
B D Sleeman and R J Jarvis
158 Hyperbolic equations
F Colombini and M K V Murthy
159 Linear topologies on a ring: an overview
J S Golan
160 Dynamical systems and bifurcation theory
M I Camacho, M J Pacifico and F Takens
161 Branched coverings and algebraic functions
M Namba
162 Perturbation bounds for matrix eigenvalues
R Bhatia
163 Defect minimization in operator equations: theory and applications
R Reemtsen
164 Multidimensional Brownian excursions and potential theory
K Burdzy
165 Viscosity solutions and optimal control
R J Elliott
166 Nonlinear partial differential equations and their applications. Collège de France Seminar. Volume VIII
H Brezis and J L Lions
167 Theory and applications of inverse problems
H Haario
168 Energy stability and convection
G P Galdi and B Straughan
169 Additive groups of rings. Volume II
S Feigelstock
170 Numerical analysis 1987
D F Griffiths and G A Watson
171 Surveys of some recent results in operator theory. Volume I
J B Conway and B B Morrel
172 Amenable Banach algebras
J-P Pier
173 Pseudo-orbits of contact forms
A Bahri
174 Poisson algebras and Poisson manifolds
K H Bhaskara and K Viswanath
175 Maximum principles and eigenvalue problems in partial differential equations
P W Schaefer
176 Mathematical analysis of nonlinear, dynamic processes
K U Grusa
177 Cordes' two-parameter spectral representation theory
D F McGhee and R H Picard
178 Equivariant K-theory for proper actions
N C Phillips
179 Elliptic operators, topology and asymptotic methods
J Roe
180 Nonlinear evolution equations
J K Engelbrecht, V E Fridman and E N Pelinovski
181 Nonlinear partial differential equations and their applications. Collège de France Seminar. Volume IX
H Brezis and J L Lions
182 Critical points at infinity in some variational problems
A Bahri
183 Recent developments in hyperbolic equations
L Cattabriga, F Colombini, M K V Murthy and S Spagnolo
184 Optimization and identification of systems governed by evolution equations on Banach space
N U Ahmed
185 Free boundary problems: theory and applications. Volume I
K H Hoffmann and J Sprekels
186 Free boundary problems: theory and applications. Volume II
K H Hoffmann and J Sprekels
187 An introduction to intersection homology theory
F Kirwan
188 Derivatives, nuclei and dimensions on the frame of torsion theories
J S Golan and H Simmons
189 Theory of reproducing kernels and its applications
S Saitoh
190 Volterra integrodifferential equations in Banach spaces and applications
G Da Prato and M Iannelli
191 Nest algebras
K R Davidson
192 Surveys of some recent results in operator theory. Volume II
J B Conway and B B Morrel
193 Nonlinear variational problems. Volume II
A Marino and M K Murthy
194 Stochastic processes with multidimensional parameter
M E Dozzi
195 Prestressed bodies
D Iesan
196 Hilbert space approach to some classical transforms
R H Picard
197 Stochastic calculus in application
J R Norris
198 Radical theory
B J Gardner
199 The C* – algebras of a class of solvable Lie groups
X Wang

200 Stochastic analysis, path integration and dynamics
D Elworthy
201 Riemannian geometry and holonomy groups
S Salamon
202 Strong asymptotics for extremal errors and polynomials associated with Erdös type weights
D S Lubinsky
203 Optimal control of diffusion processes
V S Borkar
204 Rings, modules and radicals
B J Gardner
205 Numerical studies for nonlinear Schrödinger equations
B M Herbst and J A C Weideman
206 Distributions and analytic functions
R D Carmichael and D Mitrović
207 Semicontinuity, relaxation and integral representation in the calculus of variations
G Buttazzo
208 Recent advances in nonlinear elliptic and parabolic problems
P Bénilan, M Chipot, L Evans and M Pierre
209 Model completions, ring representations and the topology of the Pierce sheaf
A Carson

The C*-algebras of a class of solvable Lie groups

Xiaolu Wang

University of Maryland

The C*-algebras of a class of solvable Lie groups

Longman Scientific & Technical

Copublished in the United States with
John Wiley & Sons, Inc., New York

Longman Scientific & Technical,
Longman Group UK Limited,
Longman House, Burnt Mill, Harlow
Essex CM20 2JE, England
and Associated Companies throughout the world.

Copublished in the United States with
John Wiley & Sons, Inc., 605 Third Avenue, New York, NY 10158

© Longman Group UK Limited 1989

All rights reserved; no part of this publication
may be reproduced, stored in a retrieval system,
or transmitted in any form or by any means, electronic,
mechanical, photocopying, recording, or otherwise,
without either the prior written permission of the Publishers
or a licence permitting restricted copying in the United Kingdom
issued by the Copyright Licensing Agency Ltd,
33-34 Alfred Place, London, WC1E 7DP.

First published 1989

AMS Subject Classification: (main) 46L55, 46M20, 43A10
(subsidiary) 46L80, 43A30, 43A55

ISSN 0269-3674

British Library Cataloguing in Publication Data
Wang, Xiaolu
The C*-algebras of a class of solvable Lie groups
1. C*-algebras
I. Title
512′.55

ISBN 0-582-03124-9

Library of Congress Cataloging-in-Publication Data
Wang, Xiaolu,
The C*-algebras of a class of solvable Lie groups
p. cm.—(Pitman research notes in mathematics series, ISSN 0269-3674; 199)
ISBN 0-470-21307-8 (Wiley)
1. C*-algebras. 2. Lie groups.
I. Title. II. Series.
QA326.W36 1989 512.'55—dc19 88-28788 CIP

Printed and bound in Great Britain
by Biddles Ltd, Guildford and King's Lynn

CStack
SCIMON

Contents

Preface

In [R1] J. Rosenberg showed that there are only finitely many C^*-algebras which arise as the group C^*-algebras of three dimensional solvable Lie groups. Of those, he characterized all but two: the C^*-algebra of the Heisenberg group, and $C^*(G_\alpha)$, $G_\alpha = G_{3,2}(-\alpha)$, $\alpha > 0$, which have the most complicated C^*-algebras. Now the C^*-algebra of the Heisenberg group is known to a fair extent (see G. G. Kasparov [K1], D. Voiculescu [V], and Gorbachef [Gor], Rosenberg [R2]), but the structure of the C^*-algebra of G_α remained mysterious.

The main result of this paper is an explicit characterization of the C^*-algebras of a class of two-step solvable Lie groups, $G(p,q,\vec{\alpha})$, $p,q = 1,2,...$, where $G(p,q,\vec{\alpha})$ is a semidirect product of a $(p+q)$ dimensional vector group with the reals. For each $t \in \mathbb{R}$, the corresponding automorphism is given by the matrix $\mathrm{diag}(e^{\alpha_1 t},...,e^{\alpha_p t}, e^{-\alpha_{p+1} t},...,e^{-\alpha_{p+q} t})$, with respect to some basis $\{e_1,...,e_{p+q}\}$, where $\alpha_i > 0$ for all i. When $p=q=1$ and $\alpha_2=1$, one obtains the family G_α in particular. The singular extensions arising from these group C^*-algebras are identified up to isomorphism with subalgebras of the multiplier algebras of the ideals. This characterization is necessary because these extensions are <u>not</u> absorbing; therefore the KK^1-elements they define do not determine them up to isomorphism. Distinct from earlier approaches, we shall work in the context of foliations, or groupoids.

In greater detail, the contents of this paper are as follows: in §0, which was added after the paper was written, we give a very sketchy outline of group C^*-algebras for nonexperts, especially mathematicians and graduate students in Lie groups, geometry and topology. What is $C^*(G)$? (and why should one say something more about it except that it is the C^*-algebra of the group G?) A similar question may be raised for a person studying $SL(n)$. No effort has been made to write a complete survey. Occasionally minor technical qualifications are suppressed in favor of clarity. Those who wish to pursue may consult the quoted references, which are often the more accessible source, rather than the original work. I apologize to those whose work should be, but is not mentioned.

In §1 we list some useful basic facts about transformation group C^*-algebras and foliations, with emphasis on their connection. Most of the fundamental properties are presented without proofs but references are given for the reader's convenience. A sketchy proof is given when the appropriate reference is not available.

In §2 we apply the results of §1 and derive various extension sequences in connection with the group C^*-algebras $C^*(G(p,q))$, which are GCR. The quotients are explicitly determined (Theorem 2.5). This extends many results in [Zep], [R1] and [Gr] in a clearer unified setting.

In §3 we follow the natural approach (as developed by Fell, Dixmier, and others) and decompose the group C^*-algebras as continuous fields of C^*-algebras over their spectrums. Combining the results from §2, we get a rough overview. The main theorem in this section is Theorem 3.1.

In §4 we study the C^*-algebras $C^*(U,\mathcal{F})$ of foliations (2.5), which is isomorphic to the transformation group C^*-algebra $C_0(U) \rtimes_\sigma \mathbb{R}$. They are C^*-algebras of homeomorphic groupoids with different left Haar systems. We compute the elements of Ext groups represented by the short exact sequences decomposing further the $C^*(U,\mathcal{F})$ into C^*-algebras with continuous trace (2.6) and obtain the structures of $C^*(U,\mathcal{F})$ in Theorems 4.3 and 4.4.

The major structure theorems are proved in 5, which are Theorems 5.24 and 5.25.

This research work (§1-§5) was written in the fall of 1984, and constituted Part I of my Ph.D. dissertation at Berkeley under the supervision of Professor Marc A. Rieffel. It could not have been written without his invaluable guidance. The wild preliminary draft covered in red marks always reminds me of the time and effort he spent. Despite his busy administrative work, Professor C. C. Moore listened patiently to my progress and caught a dangerous mistake in an early stage. Adrian Ocneanu shared his insight in a very helpful discussion concerning Theorem 4.3. During the preparation of this paper, I had many valuable conversations with William B. Arveson, Thierry Fack, and N. Chris Phillips. Jonathan Rosenberg patiently read the preliminary draft and suggested many improvements. The operator algebra year at MSRI organized by A. Connes, R. Douglas, and Takesaki made 1984-85 at Berkeley more exciting. It is my pleasure to thank all of them. I would also like to take this opportunity to acknowledge the graduate division at Berkeley for their support of a Regents Fellowship, a Wilson & Albert Flagg Fellowship and the National Science Foundation for a grant-in-aid.

X.W.

0. INTRODUCTION

A <u>C^*-algebra</u> is a Banach algebra with an involution $*$ with the crucial property that $\|x^*x\| = \|x\|^2$. The Gelfand-Naimark-Segal theorem tells us that any C^*-algebra is (isometrically $*$-isomorphic to) a norm-closed involutive subalgebra of B(H), the C^*-algebra consisting of all the bounded linear operators on a Hilbert space H. By now there are many excellent texts and reference books about C^*-algebras: [Ar 1], [Dix] [Kad], [Ped], and [Tak]. The reader may consult any of those for the basics. The <u>spectrum</u> $\hat{A}$ of a C^*-algebra A is the set of equivalence classes of irreducible $*$-representations of A with an appropriate topology. A commutative C^*-algebra always has form $C_0(\hat{A})$, the algebra of all the continuous functions on the locally compact Hausdorff space $\hat{A}$ vanishing at ∞. Thus C^*-algebras can be viewed as noncommutative "manifolds." There are C^*-algebras associated with many objects in topology and geometry, for instance, with locally compact groups. Let G be a locally compact group. The $*$-representations of $L^1(G)$ are in one to one correspondence to the unitary representations of G by the formula $\pi(f) = \int_G f(g)\pi(g)dg$. The C^*-algebra $C^*(G)$ [[Dix] p. 303] of G is defined to be the closure of the $*$-algebra $L^1(G)$ with respect to the norm $\|f\| = \sup_\pi \|\pi(f)\|$, where π ranging over all the irreducible unitary representations of G. If we complete $L^1(G)$ with respect to the norm $\|f\|_r = \|\pi_L(f)\|$, where π_L is the left regular representation, then we get the reduced group C^*-algebra $C^*_r(G)$. It follows from this definition that the spectrum $\widehat{C^*(G)}$ of the algebra $C^*(G)$ is the unitary dual $\hat{G}$ of the group G. On the one hand such a "linearization" or rather, "algebraicization," of the group representation theory provides a distinctively different point of view and made various tools in C^*-algebras available for group theorists. On the other hand it has become a rich source and an important part of operator algebras by itself. Its applications range from the proof of the classical Galfand-Raikov theorem (existence of enough irreducible unitary representations of a locally compact group to separate points [Kir]) to more recently the formulation of the index theorem for equivariant elliptic operators ([F-M], [C-M]).

A separable C^*-algebra is type I_0 (CCR, or liminary) if $\pi(A) = K(H)$ for any irreducible representation π of A on a Hilbert space H, where $K(H)$ is the algebra of all the compact operators in H. We say a separable C^*-algebra A is type I (GCR, or postliminary) if $\pi(A) \supseteq K(H)$ for all irredicible π ([Ra], [Dix]). A group is called type I_0 (or I) if its C^*-algebra is type I_0 (or I). Connected semisimple Lie groups and connected nilpotent Lie groups are type I_0 ([Dix], p. 308). Real algebraic groups are type I. On the other hand a discrete group is called type I if and only if it is essentially abelian, i.e., an extension of an abelian group by a finite group. There are solvable Lie groups which are not type I. The first such example was given by Mautner. It is a semidirect product $\mathbb{C}^2 \times_\alpha \mathbb{R}$ with $\alpha_t(\zeta_1,\zeta_2) = (e^{it}\zeta_1, e^{i\theta t}\zeta_2)$, where $t \in \mathbb{R}$ and θ is a given irrational.

The kernel of an irreducible representation of a C^*-algebra A is called a primitive ideal. The primitive ideal space of A (resp. $C^*(G)$) with the usual Jacobson topology (i.e. the hull-kernel topology) is the primitive spectrum of A (resp. G) and denoted by $\mathrm{Prim}(A)$ (resp. $\mathrm{Prim}(G)$). For any *-representation π of A, the double commutant $\pi(A)''$ is a von Neumann algebra, i.e., a *-subalgebra of $B(H)$ closed with respect to the weak *-topology. A factor is a von Neumann algebra with its center being $\mathbb{C}$. Two representations π_1 and π_2 are said to be quasi-equivalent if there is an *-isomorphism $\phi: \pi_1(A)'' \to \pi_2(A)''$ such that $\phi \circ \pi_1(x) = \pi_2(x)$ for all $x \in A$. The quasi-equivalence classes of factor representations of $C^*(G)$ form the quasi-spectrum of G, denoted by $\widehat{G}$. There are quotient maps from $\widehat{G}$ and $\hat{G}$ to Prim(G) given by $\pi \to \ker \pi$. The kernel of a factor representation is a prime ideal, which is a primitive ideal if G is separable. When G is type I, all the three spectra coincide. For non-type I groups the unitary dual $\hat{G}$ is rather "bad" (it is not T_1-separable, and is not a separable standard Borel space [Ar]). Instead of $\hat{G}$, a lot of work has been done and much is known for $\widehat{G}$, and Prim(G). Both of them are defined in terms of C^*-algebras.

For semisimple Lie group, the foundation of the theory of unitary duals $\hat{G}$ was laid by Harish-Chandra, following the beginning work of V. Bargman (SL(2,$\mathbb{R}$)) and Gelfand-Naimark (SL(2,$\mathbb{C}$), among others). For solvable Lie groups, A. A. Kirillov introduced the method of orbits ([Kir] and identified the unitary dual $\hat{G}$ with the coadjoint orbits on the dual of G for 1-connected nilpotent Lie groups. B. Kostant and L. Auslander generalized this characterization of $\hat{G}$ to all type I solvable 1-connected groups [A-K]. The difference is that the orbits Ω are no longer Euclidean spaces and for each Ω there is a family of irreducible representations of G parameterized by the characters of $\pi_1(\Omega)$. For general 1-connected solvable groups G, it is known (due to J. Glim) that in general it is impossible to explicitly determine $\hat{G}$ when G is not type I. L. Pukansky characterized Prim(G) as above but by the method of generalized orbits, which also provides a bijection from Prim(G) onto $\widehat{G}_{norm} \subset \widehat{G}$ the quasi-equivalence classes of normal representations

[Puk]. We recall more definitions. The positive cone A_+ of a C^*-algebra A is the linear span of x^*x, for all $x \in A$. A linear function (possibly taking value $\pm\infty$) τ on a von Neumann algebra is a trace if $\tau(M_+) \subset [0,\infty]$ and $\tau(xy) = \tau(yx)$ for $x,y \in M$. We say τ is faithful if $\tau(x) > 0$ for nonzero $x \in M_+$, and normal if $\tau(\sup x_i) = \sup \tau(x_i)$ for any bounded increasing net $\{x_i\}$ in M_+. A unitary representation π of G is normal if the von Neumann algebra $\pi(C^*(G))''$ has a faithful normal trace τ such that $\tau(x^*x) < \infty$ for some $x \in \pi(C^*(G))$.

C. C. Moore and J. Rosenberg [M-R] proved that for any connected Lie group G, Prim(G) is always locally T_1-separated, i.e., $C^*(G)/I$ has a unique nonzero minimal ideal M_I for every primitive ideal I. Following P. Green's work, Poguntke [P] further discovered that M_I/I is either $M_n(\mathbb{C})$ or $\mathcal{K} \otimes C^*(F_n,\nu)$ where $C^*(F_n,\nu)$ is a twisted convolution C^*-algebra of a free abelian group F_n. These C^*-algebras $C^*(F_n,\nu)$ are precisely the (higher dimensional) irrational rotation algebras studied by M. Rieffel et. al ([Rie 1], [Rie 2]).

In order to describe all the irreducible (factor) representations of $C^*(G)$ with the given kernel I, it suffices to know all the representations of M_I/I. Thus after Prim(G) is known, the classification of all irreducible representations of a Lie group is reduced to some extent to the classification of all irreducible projective representations of F_n, equivalently, the classification of irreducible modules of noncommutative tori. A major step in this direction is [Rie 2].

Not only does the study of the group C^*-algebra $C^*(G)$ provide a new approach to the study of the spectrum spaces $\hat{G}$, $\check{G}$, and Prim(G) parameterizing the representations of G, but the C^*-algebra $C^*(G)$

contains much more information about G than just these parameter spaces in the same way that a noncommutative C^*-algebra A is not at all determined by $\hat{A}$ (or A) and a bounded operator in general is by no means determined by its spectrum. Determining the structure of $C^*(G)$ or $C_r^*(G)$ has appeared to be a difficult problem even for many innocent looking groups in case they are neither abelian nor compact. For semisimple Lie groups, $C^*(G)$ is known for $CL(2,\mathbb{C})$ (Fell [F]), $SL(2,\mathbb{R})$ (Miličic [M]), the other groups with the same universal covering groups as $SL(2,\mathbb{R})$ (Kraljevic and Miličic [K-M]), and for all real rank-1 groups (Boyer and Martin [B-M], A. Valette [Val]). A. Wassermann computed the reduced C^*-algebra $C_r^*(G)$ for linear reductive Lie group [Was].

For type I groups, the theory of C^*-algebra extensions by Brown-Douglas-Fillmore (known as BDF) and Kasparov provides a powerful tool. A type I C^*-algebra A has a composition series $\{0\} = I_0 \subseteq \cdots \subseteq I_\alpha \subseteq I_{\alpha+1} \subseteq \cdots \subseteq I_\beta = A$ of closed ideals such that $I_{\alpha+1}/I_\alpha$ is a C^*-algebra of <u>continuous trace</u> and $A = \overline{\bigcup_{0\le\alpha<\beta} I_\alpha}$ ([Ped], p. 198). A continuous-trace algebra is a CCR-algebra with the property that $\{x \in A_+ \mid x \to \mathrm{Tr}\,\pi(x)$ is finite and continuous on $\hat{A}\}$ is dense in the positive cone A_+. The structures of continuous-trace algebras are well-understood ([Dix], p. 245) due to the work of Dixmier-Dourady and J. Fell. A C^*-algebra A is said to be <u>homogeneous of degree</u> n $(n=0,\ldots,\infty)$ if every irreducible representation of A is of dimension

Let X be a second countable locally compact space of finite dimension and E a locally trivial $M_n(\mathbb{C})$-bundle over X. Then the continuous cross-sections of E vanishing at ∞ constitute a continuous trace C^*-algebra of homogeneous degree n. Every continuous trace

C^*-algebra of homogeneous degree n with spectrum X arise in this way. So all such C^*-algebras are classified by the corresponding $M_n(\mathbb{C})$-bundles, namely by $[X, BPU(n)]$, or the Čech cohomology $\check{H}^1(X, \mathcal{PU}(n))$, where $\mathcal{PU}(n)$ is the sheaf of germs of continuous cross sections of a trivial $PU(n)$-bundle over X. For $n = \aleph_0$, such C^*-algebras are classified by $\check{H}^3(X,\mathbb{Z})$ $(\simeq [X, BPU(\infty)])$. The corresponding classes are called the Dixmier-Dourady invariants of the algebras. From the point of view of noncommutative topology, a type I C^*-algebra can be thought of as a <u>noncommutative CW complexes</u>, with each of these homogeneous pieces as a building block. The author studied such examples arising from foliations ([W1], [W2]). E. Effros had coined this term earlier [E]. For a nice survey of extension theory of C^*-algebras, refer [R2]. Consider an extension

$$0 \to J \to A \to B \to 0$$

of C^*-algebras. A <u>double centralizer</u> of J is a pair (ρ_1, ρ_2) of linear maps $J \to J$ such that $\rho_1(xy) = \rho_1(x)y$, $\rho_2(xy) = x\rho_2(y)$, $x\rho_1(y) = \rho_2(x)y$ for all $x,y \in J$ (cf. [Bus]). The double centralizers of J form a C^*-algebra $M(J)$, called the <u>multiplier</u> algebra of J. The quotient $O(J) = M(J)/J$ is called the <u>outer multiplier algebra</u> of J. The extension A of B by J defines a natural homomorphism $\phi\colon A \to M(J)$ taking J to itself. Thus we have a commuting diagram

$$\begin{array}{ccccccccc} 0 & \longrightarrow & J & \longrightarrow & A & \longrightarrow & B & \longrightarrow & 0 \\ & & \| & & \downarrow{\scriptstyle\phi} & & \downarrow{\scriptstyle\tau} & & \\ 0 & \longrightarrow & J & \longrightarrow & M(J) & \longrightarrow & O(J) & \longrightarrow & 0 \end{array} \qquad (0.2)$$

The homomorphism τ is called the <u>Busby invariant</u> of the extension. In some sense the most strict (or explicit) characterization of an extension (0.1) is to identify the subalgebra $\phi(A)$ of $M(J)$. A different problem, but a fundamental problem of extension theory, is: how do we distinguish all the extensions of B by J, i.e., what equivalence relations can we use? The answers are many. The Busby invariants classify the extensions according to the congruence ([Mac], p. 64, i.e. strong equivalence [Bus]) relation: (1) two extensions are congruent only if

$$\begin{array}{ccccccccc} 0 & \to & J & \to & A & \to & B & \to & 0 \\ & & \downarrow{\alpha_1} & & \downarrow{\alpha} & & \downarrow{\bar{\alpha}} & & \\ 0 & \to & J' & \to & A' & \to & B & \to & 0 \end{array} \tag{0.3}$$

with α an isomorphism and $\alpha_1 = \bar{\alpha} = \mathrm{Id}$. Weaker equivalences are (2) unitary equivalence, where α $(\bar{\alpha})$ is a conjugation by a unitary element in $M(J)$ $(O(J))$; (3) only $\bar{\alpha}$ is required to be inner automorphism; (4) in (0.3) $\alpha_1 = \mathrm{Id}$ but $\bar{\alpha}$ does not have to be inner either; (5) weak equivalence in (0.3) all the vertical isomorphisms are arbitrary as long as the diagram commutes. Of course this is just saying α is an arbitrary isomorphism from A to A'.

There are still other equivalence relations: (6) homotopy equivalence; two Busby invariants $\tau_0 \sim \tau_1$ if there is a homomorphism $\tau: A \to O(J) \otimes C[0,1]$ such that τ_0 and τ_1 are the compositions of τ with the evaluation maps at 0 and 1; (7) stable equivalence; this is by far the most useful equivalence relation, which introduces homology theory into C^*-algebras. Assume J is stable, i.e., $J \otimes K \simeq J$, so we replace J by $J \otimes K$ in (0.1). The unitary equivalence classes (2) can be made into a semigroup; the sum of two Busby invariants τ_1, τ_2 is the composite

$$B \xrightarrow{(\tau_1,\tau_2)} O(J \otimes K) \oplus O(J \otimes K) \hookrightarrow O(J \otimes K) \otimes M_2 \cong O(J \otimes K).$$

The unitary equivalence classes of split extensions, i.e., those admit *-homomorphism cross sections from B to A (see (0.1)) form a subsemigroup. The quotient is denoted by Ext(B,J) (Kasparov [Kas 1], [Kas 2]) which is a group if J has a countable approximate unit ([Ped], p. 11) and B is nuclear ([Ped], p. 393). This will always be the case when J is separable and B is type I or C^*-algebra of any connected group. Two extensions that give rise to the same element of Ext(B,J) are stably equivalent.

Distinct from all other known equivalence relations, the parameter space for the stable equivalence relations has a nice algebraic structure. (It is always a semigroup; often it is actually a group.) The Ext function for C^*-algebras was first studied by Brown-Douglas-Fillmore ([B-D-F], [D]). They were led to Ext(C(X)) (≡ Ext(C(X),ℂ)) from studying C^*-algebras generated by essentially normal operators. They discovered that Ext(C(X)) is the K-homology group $K_1(X)$. K-homology is the dual of K-theory; it also arises in the theory of elliptic operators. As in algebraic topology for manifolds, the homology invariants Ext have been shown to be powerful for describing topological structure of C^*-algebras, in particular, for group C^*-algebras. Using [B-D-F], Z'ep studied the C^*-algebra of the

$\{ax + b\}$ group over $\mathbb{R}$: $\left\{\begin{pmatrix} a & b \\ 0 & 1\end{pmatrix} : a \in \mathbb{R}^+,\ b \in \mathbb{R}\right\}$ [Z'ep].

After the discovery of K-theory, [B-D-F] marked the full-scale invasion of topology in the theory of C^*-algebras (it reciprocated afterwards, e.g., the C^*-algebra proof of the Novikov conjecture, due to Kasparov et al). Before long, Ext has been generalized to noncommutative C^*-algebras by Arveson, Effrois-Choi, and Voiculescu ([Ar 2], C-E]). Their work showed Ext(A) is again a group when A is a nuclear C^*-algebra. Pimsner-Popa-Voiculescu studied <u>homogeneous extensions</u> of A by C(X) [P-P-V], while Kasparov established the versatile KK-theory KK-bifunctor for noncommutative C^*-algebras such that $KK^1(B,J) \simeq Ext(B,J)$ as in (6). Actually Kasparov was led to this via "calculating" the C^*-algebra of a nilpotent Lie group (a problem posed to him by Kirillov): the Heisenberg group

$H_3 = \left\{ \begin{pmatrix} 1 & a & b \\ 0 & 1 & c \\ 0 & 0 & 1 \end{pmatrix}, \quad a,b,c \in \mathbb{R} \right\}$. It was not even known if the exact

sequence

$$0 \to C_0(\mathbb{R}\backslash\{0\}) \otimes \mathcal{K} \to C^*(H_3)^+ \to C(S^2) \to 0 \qquad (0.4)$$

is split (a question raised by J. Fell [Lee]). Kasparov [K1] pointed out that the exact sequence (0.4) is not stably split. For details of the proof, see [ℝ2]. Voiculescu [V] proved a stronger nonsplitting property of (0.4). For a comparision of the extension theories of Kasparov and Pimsner-Popa-Voiculescu [P-P-V], see Rosenberg and Schochet [R-S]. A very useful method of calculating KK is the universal coefficient theorem [R-S 2]. Recently R. Zekri [Zek] showed that Kasparov's Ext-theory can be defined as a C^*-algebra version of Yoneda's Ext-theory for modules [Mac]. So $Ext^n(B,J)$ consists of suitable equivalence classes of n-fold C^*-algebra extensions

$$0 \to J \otimes \mathcal{K} \to B_1 \to B_2 \to \ldots \to B_n \to B \to 0 \qquad (0.5)$$

and Kasparov's intersection product can be given by "splicing" of two exact sequences, e.g., let

$$0 \to A \otimes \quad \to J_1 \to J_2 \to \cdots \to J_m \overset{\phi}{\to} J \to 0 \tag{0.6}$$

define an element in $\mathrm{Ext}^m(J,A)$ with J stable. Then the composite $\phi' : J_m \to J \to J \otimes K$ splices (0.5) and (0.6) to a $(n+m)$-fold extension. This gives rise to the intersection product

$$\mathrm{Ext}^n(B,J) \times \mathrm{Ext}^m(J,A) \to \mathrm{Ext}^{n+m}(B,A).$$

Clearly, the problem of understanding n-fold extensions can be reduced to that for 1-fold extensions. Any n-fold extension can be obtained by splicing n 1-fold extensions.

Analogously, understanding the C^*-algebras of two-step type I solvable Lie groups is the curcial step in understanding the C^*-algebras of all type I solvable Lie groups.

Rosenberg [R1] showed that there are only finitely many C^*-algebras which arise as the group C^*-algebras of three dimensional solvable Lie groups. Again by using [B-D-F], of those he characterized all but two: the C^*-algebra of the Heisenberg group H_3 and $C^*(G_\alpha)$, $G_\alpha = G_{3,2}(-\alpha)$, $\alpha > 0$ (see [R1]), which appear to have the most complicated C^*-algebras. P. Green also studied $C^*(G)$ for several of these types of solvable Lie groups above by different techniques [G]. The C^*-algebras of the Euclidean motion groups were studied by B. Evans ([E]). Gorbachef studied $C^*(H_3)$ in [Gor]. The result of [Z'ep] has been extended to more general affine Lie groups by Varfolomeev [Va] and Son-Viet

[S-V]. However, so far $C^*(G_\alpha)$, $\alpha < 0$, remained mysterious.[†]

We say an extension σ of B by J is <u>absorbing</u> if σ is unitarily equivalent to $\sigma + \tau$ for any split extension. When $B = C(X) \otimes K$ and $J = C(Y)$, the absorbing extensions are the homogeneous extensions studied by [P-P-V]. Generalizing the result of Voiculescu, Kasparov showed that in every stable equivalence class, there is an absorbing extension, which is clearly unique up to unitary equivalence. By Connes' isormorphism [C1] and the six term exact sequence, it is quite easy to compute the KK^1-elements defined by the extension associated to $C^*(G_\alpha)$ (cf. Example 4.11). From the nonvanishing of the KK^1-elements, one concludes that these extensions are not stably split. Unfortunately these elements in KK^1 (or Ext) groups do not determine the C^*-algebras $C^*(G_\alpha)$, because these extensions are <u>not</u> absorbing (they are <u>singular</u> extensions). This is the real difficulty. In this paper we identify $C^*(G_\alpha)$ explicitly with a subalgebra of M(J) (Theorems 5.24, 5.25), thereby characterizing $C^*(G_\alpha)$ among all the extensions of B by J up to isomorphism and therefore completely solving the problem. As we mentioned earlier, it is another problem to classify all the extensions of B by J according to various equivalence relations, finer than the stable equivalence relation. If the parameter space of classification admits some

---

† This paper was written in the fall, 1984. As the paper was being typed, the author received by mail a manuscript [Viet], which is concerned with $G_{3,2}(-\alpha)$. There are two main theorems in [V]. One of them obtains that the exact sequences (2.9) and (2.11) are exact in the case p = q = 1; see (2.8) and (2.10). The other computes elements of KK^1-groups associated to the extension, see Example 4.11.

algebraic structure, and is computable, so much the better. In general if two extensions of B by J are known, i.e., identified with subalgebras of M(J), then one can see if they are different with respect to various equivalence relations.

The main results are Theorems 5.23, 5.24 and 5.25. Theorem 5.24 and the last statement of 5.25, i.e., the construction of the cross sections from B to M(J) ($J = C^*(U_1, F)$, cf. (2.8)), is the crucial part. Although there are shorter direct proofs for some statements (e.g., i), ii) of Theorem 5.23) by using [Ake]), the explicit calculations omitted would still have to be taken up for the rest.

Throughout this paper, as usual, we denote $\mathcal{K}(H)$ to be the C^*-algebra of compact operators on a separable Hilbert space H. Denote $\mathcal{L}(H)$ the C^*-algebra of all bounded operators on H. Let A be any C^*-algebra, we denote its unitalization by A^+. For a locally compact space X, we denote by $C_0(X,A)$ the C^*-algebra of norm continuous functions from X to A vanishing at ∞. We denote by $C^b(X,A)$ all bounded norm continuous functions from X to A, and by $C^b_{*-s}(X,A)$ all bounded $*$-strong continuous functions from X to A when A is represented in a Hilbert space H. The $n \times n$ matrix algebra with entries in a C^*-algebra A is denoted by $M_n(A)$. It is embedded in $\mathcal{L}(H \oplus \ldots \oplus H)$ in an obvious way if $A \subset \mathcal{L}(H)$.

§1. PRELIMINARIES

The solvable Lie groups we are concerned with have a Lie algebra $\mathcal{G}$ of the following type: with appropriate choice it has a basis $\{e_1, e_2, \ldots, e_{n+1}\}$ where $\{e_1, e_2, \ldots, e_n\}$ is a basis for an abelian ideal $\mathcal{N}$ of $\mathcal{G}$ and e_{n+1} acts on $\mathcal{N}$ diagonally by the adjoint representation

$$[e_{n+1}, e_i] = \alpha_i e_i, \qquad \alpha_i \in \mathbb{R}, \qquad i = 1, \ldots, n .$$

If certain $\alpha_i = 0$, say $\alpha_n = 0$, then it is easy to see that the corresponding simply connected Lie group has a decomposition $G \simeq \mathbb{R}^n \times \mathbb{R} \simeq (\mathbb{R}^{n-1} \times \mathbb{R}) \times \mathbb{R}$ where the factor $\mathbb{R}^{n-1}$ in the semidirect product has generators $e_1, e_2, \ldots, e_{n-1}$. Thus there is a decomposition for its C^*-algebra:

$$C^*(G) \simeq C^*(\mathbb{R}^{n-1} \rtimes \mathbb{R}) \otimes C^*(\mathbb{R}) \simeq C^*(\mathbb{R}^{n-1} \rtimes \mathbb{R}) \otimes C_0(\mathbb{R}) ,$$

therefore we may assume that all $\alpha_i \neq 0$ without loss of generality.
In this paper we study the corresponding solvable Lie groups $G(p,q,\vec{\alpha})$, $p,q = 1,2,\ldots$, where $G(p,q,\vec{\alpha})$ is a semidirect product of a (p+q) dimensional vector group with the reals. For each $t \in \mathbb{R}$, the corresponding automorphism is given by the matrix $\mathrm{diag}(e^{\alpha_1 t},\ldots,e^{\alpha_p t},e^{-\alpha_{p+1} t},\ldots,e^{-\alpha_{p+q} t})$ with respect to some basis $\{e_1,\ldots,e_{p+q}\}$, where $\alpha_i > 0$ for all i.
When p=q=1 and $\alpha_2 = 1$, one obtains the family $G_\alpha = G_{3,2}(-\alpha)$, $\alpha > 0$ in [R1].

Note that the C*-algebra of $G(p,q,\vec{\alpha})$ is the same as that of the topological transformation group $(\mathbb{R},\mathbb{R}^{p+q})$, with the $\mathbb{R}$-action given by the matrix $\mathrm{diag}(e^{\alpha_1 t},\ldots,e^{\alpha_p t},e^{-\alpha_{p+1} t},\ldots,e^{-\alpha_{p+q} t})$, dual to the $\mathbb{R}$-action in the semi-direct product. When all $\alpha_i = 1$, we denote the group by G(p,q). It is easy to see that the lengths of the roots α_i do not affect the structure of C*-algebras. Thus one needs only to consider the family $\{G(p,q)\}$.

For the basic facts about C*-algebras of transformation groups and crossed products, the reader is referred to Effros and Hahn [E-H] and Pedersen [Ped]. A very useful fact about crossed products is (see Lemma 1.1 [C1]):

PROPOSITION 1.1. *Let* $0 \to I \to A \to B \to 0$ *be an* $\mathbb{R}$*-equivariant exact sequence of* C**-algebras. Then we have a corresponding exact sequence of crossed products*

(1.1) $$0 \to I \rtimes \mathbb{R} \to A \rtimes \mathbb{R} \to B \rtimes \mathbb{R} \to 0$$

(When $\mathbb{R}$ *is replaced by a arbitrary locally compact group* G *the assertion remains true.)*

In particular, for a transformation group $(V,\mathbb{R}^k)$, if U is an invariant open subset of V, then

(1.2) $$0 \longrightarrow C_0(U) \times \mathbb{R}^k \longrightarrow C_0(V) \times \mathbb{R}^k \longrightarrow C_0(V\setminus U) \times \mathbb{R}^k \longrightarrow 0 \quad .$$

If $(V,\mathbb{R}^k)$ is a smooth transformation group, then a foliation of V arises in many situations. A good introduction to foliations is B.Lawson's [L]. Here we give the basic definitions for the sake of completeness.

By definition, a codimension q foliation on a smooth n-manifold is a decomposition of V into a disjoint union $V = \bigcup_{\alpha\in\Lambda} L_\alpha$ of leaves such that

i) each L_α is a smooth connected (n-q)-submanifold of V.

ii) locally the L_α's are the fibres of a smooth submersion.

More explicitly, for any $x \in V$, there is a coordinate patch (U,ϕ) such that $\phi(U)$ is the unit cube in $\mathbb{R}^n$ and $\{\phi(L_\alpha \cap U)\}$ are given by $x_1 = \text{const.},\ldots,x_q = \text{const.}$ We call U a *fundamental neighborhood* and call the $L_\alpha \cap U$ *plaques*.

Let $\gamma\colon [0,1] \rightarrow L$ be a path in a leaf L. Take small fundamental neighborhoods U_1 and U_2 and local transversals N_1 and N_2 of $\gamma(0)$ and $\gamma(1)$ respectively, such that each plaque $L_\alpha \cap U_i$ intersects N_i only at one point. Then the *holonomy map* $\phi_{\gamma(0),\gamma(1)}$ is the germ of the diffeomorphism mapping N_1 to N_2 obtained by, roughly speaking, translating plaques onto plaques along the leaves.

Let Γ be the groupoid of paths along leaves of $\mathcal{F}$, with composition given by concatenation. Define an equivalence relation $\simeq$ on Γ by $\gamma_1 \simeq \gamma_2$ iff $\gamma_1(0) = \gamma_2(0)$, $\gamma_1(1) = \gamma_2(1)$ and $\gamma_1\gamma_2^{-1}$ induces trivial holonomy at $\gamma_1(0)$. Then the *graph* (i.e. the *holonomy groupoid*) $\mathbb{G}$ is by definition the quotient $\Gamma/\simeq$.

The C^*-algebra of foliation $C^*(V,\mathcal{F})$ was defined by A.Connes [C1].

It can be considered as the reduced C*-algebra of the holonomy groupoid G. For the definitions of groupoids and their associated C*-algebras, see [Ren]. When $\mathbb{G}$ is Hausdorff, let $C_c^\infty(\mathbb{G}, \Omega^{\frac{1}{2}})$ denote the smooth half densities with compact support on $\mathbb{G}$. We can choose a metric on the tangent bundle $T\mathcal{F}$ of the foliation $\mathcal{F}$ such that the metric gives a cross section of $(\Omega_x^{\frac{1}{2}})_{x \in V}$, so that $C_c^\infty(\mathbb{G}, \Omega^{\frac{1}{2}})$ is identified with $C_c^\infty(\mathbb{G})$. When $\mathbb{G}$ is not Hausdorff, $C_c^\infty(\mathbb{G})$ is defined to be all the linear combinations of functions $\phi \circ \chi$ where $\chi: U \longrightarrow \mathbb{R}^{n+p}$ is a local chart for $\mathbb{G}$ and $\phi \in C_c^\infty(\mathbb{R}^{n+p})$ with $\mathrm{supp}(\phi) \subset \chi(U)$.

For $f,g \in C_c^\infty(\mathbb{G})$, we define the convolution product $f*g$ by

(1.3) $$(f*g)(\gamma) = \int_{\gamma_1\gamma_2=\gamma} f(\gamma_1)g(\gamma_2) \quad , \qquad \gamma \in \mathbb{G}$$

and involution

(1.4) $$f^*(\gamma) = \bar{f}(\gamma^{-1}) \quad .$$

With this operation $C_c^\infty(\mathbb{G}, \Omega^{\frac{1}{2}})$ is a *-algebra. For each leaf L_α, there is a natural representation of $C_c^\infty(\mathbb{G}, \Omega^{\frac{1}{2}})$ on $L^2(\tilde{L}_\alpha)$, where $\tilde{L}_\alpha$ is the holonomy covering of L. Let $x \in L_\alpha$, and identify $\tilde{L}_\alpha$ with $\mathcal{G}_x = \{\gamma \in \mathbb{G} | s(\gamma) = x\}$. Then the representation π_x is defined by

(1.5) $$\pi_x(f)(\xi)(\gamma) = \int_{\gamma_1\gamma_2 = \gamma} f(\gamma_1)\xi(\gamma_2), \qquad \xi \in L_2(\mathbb{G}_x, \Omega^{\frac{1}{2}})$$

for each $f \in C_c^\infty(\mathbb{G}, \Omega^{\frac{1}{2}})$.

<u>Definition 1.2</u>. $C^*(V,\mathcal{F})$ is the completion of $C_c(\mathbb{G},\Omega^{\frac{1}{2}})$ with respect to the norm

$$\|f\| = \sup_x \|\pi_x(f)\|$$

where x ranges over all leaves.

We now list several basic propositions which will be used frequently in the following sections.

PROPOSITION 1.3. *If the foliation is given by a submersion* $p: V \to M$, *then its graph is* $\mathbb{G} = \{(x,y) \in V \times V \mid p(x) = p(y)\}$, $C^*(V, \mathcal{F}) \simeq C_0(M) \otimes \mathcal{K}(L^2(L_\alpha))$ *where* L_α *is any leaf.*

PROPOSITION 1.4. *If the foliation* $(V,\mathcal{F})$ *comes from an action* τ *of a Lie group* H *such that the graph* $\mathbb{G}$ *naturally identifies with* $V \times H$, *then* $C^*(V,\mathcal{F}) \simeq C_0(V) \times_\tau H$.

PROPOSITION 1.5. *Let* $U \subset V$ *be a saturated open set. Then* $C^*(U,\mathcal{F})$ *is an ideal of* $C^*(V,\mathcal{F})$. *Let* $X = V \backslash U$. *If the foliation of* X *arises from an action of* $\mathbb{R}^k \times T^\ell$ *in such a way that its graph is* $X \times (\mathbb{R}^k \times T^\ell)$, *then*

$$0 \to C^*(U,\mathcal{F}) \to C^*(X,\mathcal{F}) \to C^*(V,\mathcal{F}) \to 0$$

is exact.

A proof of Proposition 1.5 can be found in Torpe's thesis (Lemma 2.2.1 [Tor]), where a stronger fact is proved.

There is a very close relation between transformation groups and foliations. In fact, given any differentiable transformation group (V,H) such that the isotropy subgroup, H_x, at x, has the same dimension for all $x \in V$, the orbits of H form a foliation of V (see [L], p.5).

Assume this ; let's remove the assumption about the graph of the foliation in 1.4 and examine the relations between the transformation groupoid and the graph of the corresponding foliation as well as the relation between their C*-algebras in general situation.

When a foliation is induced by a group action, holonomy maps can be described in a particularly explicit way.

LEMMA 1.6. *Assume that the foliation* $(V,\mathcal{F})$ *comes from a smooth action* α *of a connected Lie group* H. *Let* γ *be a path in* H *starting at* e, *the identity element of* H, *and ending at* h. *Let* $\gamma' = \alpha_{\gamma(\cdot)}(x)$ *be the corresponding path in* V *such that* $\gamma'(0) = x$ *and* $\gamma'(1) = y$. *Let* T_x *be a smooth transversal containing* x. *Then* $\gamma(1)(T_x)$ *is a transversal containing* y *and a representative of the holonomy germ* $[\gamma'] \in \mathbb{G}_x^y$ *is given by the mapping* $P \to \gamma(1)P$ *for* $P \in T_x$.

Proof. Let U_x be an open fundamental neighborhood of x. We may assume $T_x \subset U_x$ as we are only interested in the germs of the holonomy map.

For each $t \in [0,1]$, $\alpha_{\gamma(t)}$ is a diffeomorphism mapping a neighborhood of x onto a neighborhood of $\alpha_{\gamma(t)}(x)$. It preserves the orbits therefore maps plaques onto plaques and transversals to transversals. Since γ is compact, for small transversal T_x we can pick $0 = t_0 < t_1 < \dots < t_n = 1$ such that (i) $\{\alpha_{\gamma(t_i)}U_x\}_{i=0,\dots,n}$ covers γ'; (ii) the transversal $T_i = \alpha_{\gamma(t_i')}T_x$ is contained in $\alpha_{\gamma(t_i)}(U_x) \cap \alpha_{\gamma(t_{i+1})}(U_x)$ for some $t_i' \in (t_i, t_{i+1})$, $i = 0,\dots,n-1$. Now by definition, a holonomy map sends T to T_1 by mapping P to $\alpha_{\gamma(t_i')}(P)$. For $i = 0,\dots,n-1$, a holonomy map from T_i to T_{i+1} by taking $\alpha_{\gamma(t_i')}(P)$ to $\alpha_{\gamma(t_{i+1}')}(P)$. Iterating this we get a holonomy map from T to $\gamma(1)(T_x)$ described as in the lemma. Q.E.D.

LEMMA 1.7. *Assume the notations in Lemma 1.6. Let* Ω *be a loop in* H *based at* e *and* $\Omega' = \alpha_{\Omega(\cdot)}(x)$. *Then* Ω' *represents the trivial element in* $\mathbb{G}_x^x$.

Proof. It follows immediately from Lemma 1.6. Q.E.D.

PROPOSITION 1.8. *Assume that the foliation* $(V, \mathcal{F})$ *comes from a smooth action* α *of a connected Lie group* H. *Then for each* $x \in V$ *there is a natural homomorphism* ϕ_x *from the isotropy subgroup* H_x *onto the holonomy group* G_x^x *of the leaf* L_x. *Moreover* ϕ_x *annihilates the connected component* H_x^0 *of the identity in* H_x *and induces a canonical epimorphism*

$$\phi_x' : H_x/H_x^0 = \pi_0(H_x) \longrightarrow \mathbb{G}_x^x .$$

Proof. For $h \in H_x$, let $\gamma: [0,1] \to H$ be a path in H starting at e. The identity element of H, and ending at h. Then $\gamma' = \alpha_{\gamma(\cdot)}(x)$ is a loop in V based at x which gives an element $[\gamma']$ in $\mathbb{G}_x^x$ by Lemma 1.6.

Let γ_1 be another path connecting e and h. Consider the usual composition of paths $\Omega = \gamma_1^{-1} * \gamma$ which is a loop in H based at e. By Lemma 1.7, $\Omega' = \alpha_{\Omega(\cdot)}(x)$ represents the trivial element in $\mathbb{G}_x^x$. Hence $[\gamma_1'] = [\gamma']$ and it depends only on h and we can denote it by $\phi_x(h)$.

Assume for $h_i \in H_x$ that the above construction provides a path γ_i in H with $\gamma_i(0) = e$, $\gamma_i(1) = h_i$ and a loop γ_i', $\phi_x(h_i) = [\gamma_i'] \in \mathbb{G}_x^x$, for $i = 1,2$. See Figure 1.1. Since

$$\alpha_{\gamma_1(t)h_2}(x) = \alpha_{\gamma_1(t)}(\alpha_{h_2}(x)) = \alpha_{\gamma_1(t)}(x) = \gamma_1'(t) ,$$

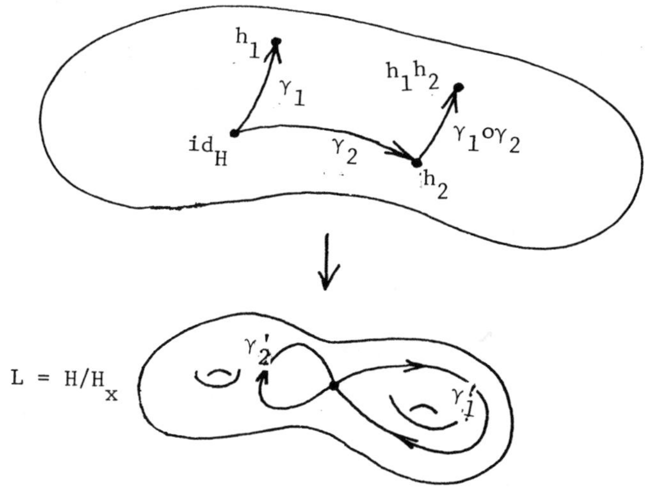

Figure 1.1

we see that $\gamma_1(\cdot)h_2$ is a lift of γ_1' starting at h_2 and ending at h_1h_2.

Let γ be the path in H obtained by composing γ_2 followed by $\gamma_1(\cdot)\cdot h_2$. Then we have

$$\phi_x(h_1h_2) = [\gamma'] = [(\gamma_1 h_2 * \gamma_2)'] = [(\gamma_1 h_2)' * \gamma_2']$$

$$= [\gamma_1' * \gamma_2'] = [\gamma_1'][\gamma_2'] = \phi_x(h_1)\phi_x(h_2) .$$

Hence $\phi_x\colon H_x \to \mathbb{G}_x^x$ is a group homomorphism. Note that both H and $\mathbb{G}_x^x$ can be nonabelian so the order is important.

Clearly ϕ_x is onto. For let a loop γ' represent an element of $\mathbb{G}_x^x$. Then there is a path γ in H such that $\alpha_{\gamma(\cdot)}(x) = \gamma'$, $\gamma(0) = e$. If $h = \gamma(1)$, then $h \in H_x$ and $\phi_x(h) = [\gamma']$.

Finally, if h_1 and h_2 are in the same connected component of H_x then $\phi_x(h_1) = \phi_x(h_2)$. Q.E.D.

<u>Remark 1.9</u>. There is a natural quotient map q from the fundamental group $\pi_1(L_x,x) \longrightarrow \mathbb{G}_x^x$, for every $x \in V$. Under the assumption of Proposition 1.8 there is a canonical commutative diagram:

$$\begin{array}{ccccc} H_x & \longrightarrow & H_x/H_x^0 & \xrightarrow{\ \simeq\ } & \pi_1(H/H_x,x) \\ & \searrow^{\phi_x} & \downarrow{\scriptstyle \phi_x'} & & \Vert \\ & & \mathbb{G}_x^x & \xleftarrow{\ q\ } & \pi_1(L_x,x) \end{array}$$

Recall that a transformation group is called *locally free* if the isotropy groups are all discrete.

PROPOSITION 1.10. *Assume that the foliation* $(V,\mathcal{F})$ *comes from a smooth action* α *of a connected Lie group* H. *Then the graph of foliation* $\mathbb{G}$ *is a quotient groupoid of the transformation groupoid, i.e. there is a submersion* ϕ *from* $V \times H$ *onto* $\mathbb{G}$ *preserving the groupoid operation. If the* H-*action is locally free, then* ϕ *is a covering map.*

<u>Proof</u>. For $(x,h) \in V \times H$, we define $\phi(x,h) = (x, \alpha_h(x), [\gamma']) \in \mathbb{G}$, where $[\gamma']$ is described as in Lemma 1.6. By Lemma 1.6 and Proposition 1.8, ϕ is well defined and preserves the law of groupoid composition. It is straightforward to check that ϕ is a submersion from manifold $V \times H$ onto $\mathbb{G}$. The rest is clear. Q.E.D.

<u>Remark</u>. In many cases (for example, if ϕ is proper) the quotient

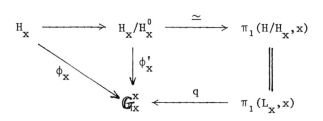

groupoid homomorphism ϕ induces an embedding from $C^*(U,\mathcal{G})$ into $C_0(U) \rtimes H$. The maps $\phi_0 = \{\phi_x\}$ constructed in Lemma 1.8 is a group bundle homomorphism ([Ren], p. 7) from the isotropy group bundle of the transformation groupoid $V \times H$ onto the isotropy group bundle of the holonomy groupoid $\mathbb{G}$.

PROPOSITION 1.11. *The map* ϕ_0 *is an isomorphism from the isotropy group bundle* $\{H_x\}$ *onto the holonomy group bundle* $\{\mathbb{G}_x^x\}$ *if and only if the map* ϕ *is an isomorphism of groupoids.*

Proof. Suppose that ϕ is not an isomorphism of topological groupoids. There are (x,h_1) and (x,h_2) in $V \times H$ such that $(x, \alpha_{h_1}(x), [\gamma_1']) = (x, \alpha_{h_2}(x), [\gamma_2'])$. Thus $\phi_x(h_2^{-1} \cdot h_1) = [\gamma_2'^{-1}][\gamma_1] = \mathrm{id} \in \mathbb{G}_x^x$. The assumption that $\phi_0 = \{\phi_x\}$ is isomorphic implies that $h_2^{-1} \cdot h_1 = e$ and $(x,h_1) = (x,h_2)$.

The opposite direction is obvious. Q.E.D.

Note that the assertion of Proposition 1.11 is true for an epimorphism ϕ of topological groupoids and the restriction ϕ_0 of ϕ on the isotropy group bundles. The proof of Proposition 1.11 can be repeated for this generality.

PROPOSITION 1.12. *Assume that* (H,V) *is a smooth transformation group, both* H *and* V *are connected, and the action* α *of* H *is locally free on* $U = V \backslash F$, *where* F *is the closed subset of* V *consisting of fixed points. Then the action of* H *restricted to* U *induces a foliation* $(U,\mathcal{F})$. *If in addition the* ϕ_x' *is injective for every* $x \in U$ *(see Remark 1.9), then we have an exact sequence*

$$0 \longrightarrow C^*(U,\mathcal{F}) \to C_0(V) \rtimes_{r,\alpha} H \longrightarrow C_0(F) \otimes C_r^*(H) \longrightarrow 0$$

Proof. It is clear that U is an invariant open subset of V, and that $C_0(F) \rtimes_{r,\alpha} H \simeq C_0(F) \otimes C_r^*(H)$ as the α-action is trivial on F. So by Proposition 1.1,

$$0 \longrightarrow C_0(U) \rtimes_{r,\alpha} H \longrightarrow C_0(V) \rtimes_{r,\alpha} H \longrightarrow C_0(F) \otimes C_r^*(H) \longrightarrow 0 \quad .$$

The α-action of H on U induces a foliation. By Proposition 1.10, there is a groupoid homomorphism ϕ from $U \times H$ onto the graph $\mathbb{G}(U,\mathcal{F})$. If in addition ϕ_x' is injective, then by Proposition 1.11 $U \times H$ is isomorphic to $\mathbb{G}(U,\mathcal{F})$. From Proposition 1.3 we conclude that $C_0(U) \rtimes_{r,\alpha} H \simeq C^*(U,\mathcal{F})$. Q.E.D.

Of course Proposition 1.12 applies trivially if the H-action on U is free. The foliation of two-torus consisting of two copies of orientation reversing Reeb components induced by an $\mathbb{R}$-action is a nontrivial simple example of ϕ_x being injective, for x on the compact leaves. See Figure 1.2. Another example is given by a Möbius strip, which is a vector bundle over S^1, with a fibre-transversal foliation induced by an S^1-action. For x on the central line, we have $H_x \simeq G_x^x \simeq \mathbb{Z}_2$ (Figure 1.3).

Suppose that the two-torus is foliated by an even number of orientation-reversing Reeb components separating each other by compact stable leaves (see [C2], p.567). Then the foliation is induced by an

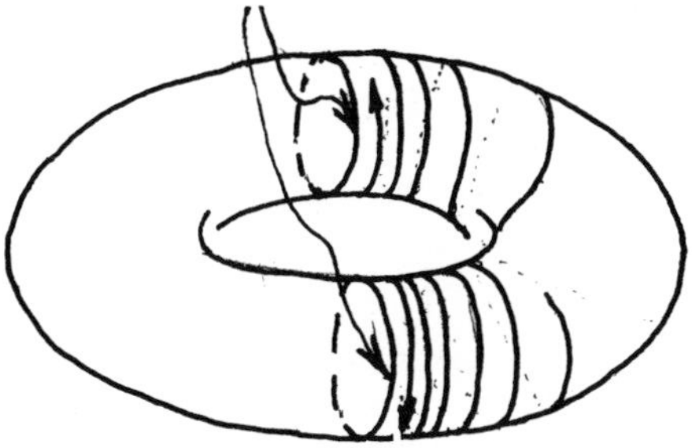

Figure 1.2

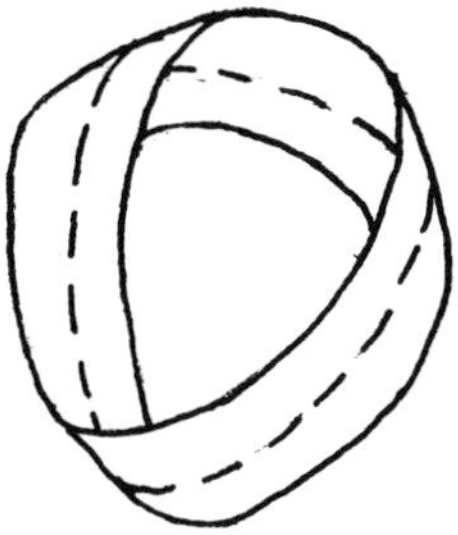

Figure 1.3

$\mathbb{R}$-action. Note that for every x on a compact stable leaf the holonomy group G_x^x is trivial but $H_x \simeq \mathbb{Z}$. Thus ϕ_x fails to be injective and the C*-algebra of the foliation is substantially different from the transformation group C*-algebra. So $K_*(C^*(T,\mathcal{F}))$ can have an arbitrarily large number of generators when the number of Reeb components gets large. See [C2, p.570] and [Tor].

Another example for which $\phi_0 = \{\phi_x\}$ in Proposition 1.12 fails to be injective is the group $G_{3,4}(0)$; see Figure 1, (1c) of [R1, p.182].

2. THE EXTENSIONS AND SUBQUOTIENT ALGEBRAS

First we closely examine the special case that all roots are positive, so the groups are of the form $G(m,0) = \mathbb{R}^m \rtimes \mathbb{R}$. The C*-algebras of these type of groups have been studied by Rosenberg [R1]. Based on the results of [R1], the explicit expression of the C*-algebra of $G(m,0)$ is given in Theorem 2.1.

In the general case, we shall study the structure of the group C^*-algebra $C^*(G(p,q))$ via two exact sequences (2.5) and (2.9). In this section the structure of the quotient in (2.9) is given in Theorem 2.2, which includes the conclusion of Theorem 2.1 as a special case. In particular, it generalizes and interprets some results [Zép], [Gr] and [R1] in a uniform setting.

Let us recall the following result of Rosenberg about $G(m,0)$ [R1]. The multiplication in $G(m,0)$ is given by the formula

$$(x_1,\ldots,x_{m+1})(y_1,\ldots,y_{m+1}) = (x_1+y_1 \exp x_{m+1},\ldots,x_m+y_n \exp x_{m+1},\ x_{m+1}+y_{m+1})$$

There is an exact sequence

$$(2.1) \qquad 0 \to C(S^{m-1}, \mathcal{K}) \to C^*(G(m,0))^+ \to C(S^1) \to 0$$

where $C(S^{m-1},\mathcal{K}) \simeq C_0(\mathbb{R}^m\setminus\{0\}) \rtimes \mathbb{R}$, ([R1], (2)). Lét $g \in L^1(G(m,0)) \subset C^*(G(m,0))$. For $\zeta \in S^{m-1}$, $f \in L^2(\mathbb{R})$, let

$$(\pi_\zeta(g)f)(s) = \int_{\mathbb{R}} f(s-t)\tilde{g}(e^{-S}\zeta,\ t)dt \quad ,$$

where $\tilde{g}$ is the Fourier transform of g in the first m variables. Then the mapping $g \mapsto (\pi \mapsto \pi_\zeta(g))$ gives an embedding μ of $C^*(G(m,0))$ into $C(S^{m-1}, B(H))$, and the Busby invariant $\gamma\colon C(S^1) \to C(S^{m-1}, B(H)/K(H))$ has an image consisting of constant functions $S^{m-1} \to B(H)/K(H)$. Recall that for an extension of C^*-algebras ([R1], Prop. 4),

$$0 \to I \to A \to B \to 0 \quad .$$

the Busby invariant is the homomorphism from B into $M(I)/I$ induced by multiplication by elements of A [Bus].

Thus the extension (2.1) is determined by an element of $\mathrm{Ext}(S^1) \simeq \mathbb{Z}$ (see [B-D-F] and also [D], Thm. 2). Rosenberg then showed that for a preimage $1+g$ in $C^*(\mathbb{G}(m,0))$ of a positive generator of $K_1(C(S^1))$ ([R1], p.186), the Fredholm index of $1+\pi_\zeta(g)$ is -1 for all $\zeta \in S^{m-1}$ ([R1], Prop. 5), so the isomorphism class of $C^*(G(m,0))$ is uniquely determined ([R1], p.186-187).

From the above result by Rosenberg, we easily derive an explicit characterization of the group C^*-algebra $C^*(G(m,0))$.

THEOREM 2.1. *Let* S *be a unilateral shift operator in a separable Hilbert space* H *and* $\tau\colon C^*(S) \to C(S^1)$ *be the quotient map (see, for instance* [D], p.4*). Then*

$$C^*(G(0,m))^+ \simeq \{f \in C(S^{m-1}, C^*(S)) \mid \tau(f(\zeta)) \in C(S^1) \textit{ is independent of } \zeta \in S^{m-1}\} .$$

<u>Proof</u>. From the proof of Proposition 3 [R1], it is easy to see that the image of the representation π_ζ of $C^*(G(m,0))$ is $C^*(\pi_\zeta(a))$, and the $C^*(\pi_\zeta(a))$ are identical for all $\zeta \in S^{m-1}$. Since the Fredholm index of $I+\pi_\zeta(a)$ is -1, there is an isomorphism α from $C^*(\pi_\zeta(a))^{-1}$ onto $C^*(S)$ (cf. [D], Thm.2, p.9) and the following diagram commutes:

$$\begin{array}{ccccccccc} 0 & \longrightarrow & \mathcal{K} & \longrightarrow & C^*(\pi_\zeta(a))^+ & \longrightarrow & C(S^1) & \longrightarrow & 0 \\ & & \| & & \downarrow{\scriptstyle\alpha} & & \| & & \\ 0 & \longrightarrow & \mathcal{K} & \longrightarrow & C^*(S) & \longrightarrow & C(S^1) & \longrightarrow & 0 \end{array}$$

The isomorphism α gives rise to an isomorphism α' from $C(S^{m-1}, C^*(\pi_\zeta(a))^+)$ to $C(S^{m-1}, C^*(S))$. We set $\mu' = \tilde{\alpha}\cdot\mu^+$. Recall that μ is an embedding of $C^*(G(m,0))$ into $C(S^{m-1}, B(H))$ and μ^+ is the extension of μ. Clearly μ' embeds $C^*(G(m,0))^+$ into $\{f \in C(S^{m-1}, C(S^*)) \mid \tau(f(\zeta)) \in C(S^1)$ is independent of $\zeta\}$, because of an earlier remark about the Busby invariant γ.

We use a C*-algebraic version of the Stone-Weierstrass theorem to show that the imbedding μ' is onto. Since the algebra A_m on the right side of (2.2) is a GCR C*-algebra, one needs only to check that $C^*(G(m,0))^+$ is a rich C*-subalgebra of A_m (cf. [Dix], 11.1.1). Here we identify $C^*(G(m,0))^+$ with its image through μ'.

Inequivalent irreducible representations of A_m are parametrized by $(\zeta,\alpha) \in S^{m-1} \times \widehat{C^*(S)}$. From the proof of Proposition 4 [R1], for each $T \in C^*(S)$, the constant function on S^{m-1} with value T is in $C^*(G(m,0))^+$. Therefore for every irreducible representation $\pi = (\rho,\alpha)$ of A_m, the restriction of π to $C^*(G(m,0))^+$ is still irreducible. Suppose $\pi_i = (\zeta_i,\alpha_i)$, i=1,2, are two inequivalent irreducible representations of A_m. Note that (ζ_1,λ) is unitarily equivalent to (ζ_2,α) for all $\zeta_1,\zeta_2 \in S^{m-1}$ and $\alpha \in S^1 \subset \widehat{C^*(S)}$, so we are left with the following three situations:

(i) $\alpha_1 \neq \alpha_2$, where α_1,α_2 are in S^1; $\zeta_1,\zeta_2 \in S^{m-1}$.

Thus π_1,π_2 are one-dimensional. With the same notation as in the proof of Proposition 4 [R1], for the element $a = 1+g$ in $C^*(G(m,0))^+$, $\lambda \to U_\lambda(a) = (i\lambda+1)/(i\lambda-1)$ is a homeomorphism sending $\mathbb{R} \cup \{\infty\}$ onto S^1 with winding number 1. There are $\lambda_1 \neq \lambda_2$, such that $U_{\lambda_i}(a) = \alpha_i$, i=1,2. Recall the definition of the embedding μ', we have $\pi_1(a) = U_{\lambda_1}(a) \neq U_{\lambda_2}(a) = \pi_2(a)$. Thus $\pi_1|C^*(G(m,0))^+ \not\sim \pi_2|C^*(G(m,0))^+$.

(ii) $\alpha_1 \in S^1$, $\alpha_2 = id_{C^*(S)}$, $\zeta_1,\zeta_2 \in S^{m-1}$.

Again $\pi_1(a) = \alpha_1 \in \mathbb{C}$ is of course not unitarily equivalent to

$\pi_2(a) = \pi_{\zeta_2}(g) + I$, which is an operator of Fredholm index 1. Thus the restriction of π_1 and π_2 are not unitarily equivalent.

(iii) $\alpha_1 = \alpha_2 = id_{C^*(S)}$ but $\zeta_1 \neq \zeta_2$ in S^{m-1}.
There exists $f \in C(S^{m-1}, \mathcal{K}) \subset C^*(G(m,0))$ such that $f(\zeta_1) = 0$ but $f(\zeta_2) \neq 0$. Then $\pi_1(f) = f(\zeta_1)$ and $\pi_2(f) = f(\zeta_2)$ are not unitarily equivalent.

Thus $C^*(G(m,0))^+$ is a rich C*-subalgebra of A_m, so we can apply 11.1.6 of [Dix]. Q.E.D.

We now start the investigation of the C*-algebras of the solvable Lie groups G(p,q) defined in §1. Consider the corresponding transformation groups $(\mathbb{R}^{p+q}, \mathbb{R})$ with the dual group actions. There is a fixed point $F = \{0\}$. Let $U = \mathbb{R}^{p+q} \setminus \{0\}$ be the $\mathbb{R}$-action on U and is free and induces a foliation $(U, \mathcal{F})$. By Proposition 1.1 there is an exact sequence

$$(2.4) \qquad 0 \to C_0(U) \rtimes_\sigma \mathbb{R} \to C_0(\mathbb{R}^{p+q}) \rtimes_\sigma \mathbb{R} \to C_0(\mathbb{R}) \to 0 .$$

By Proposition 1.4 we know that there *exists* some *abstract* isomorphism between $C_0(U) \rtimes_\sigma \mathbb{R}$ and $C^*(U, \mathcal{F})$. Considering the unitalization of (2.4), we have

$$(2.5) \qquad 0 \to C^*(U, \mathcal{F}) \to C^*(G(p,q))^+ \xrightarrow{\pi_0} C(S^1) \to 0 .$$

We will determine the structure of $C^*(U, \mathcal{F})$ in §4 and construct an isomorphism from $C_0(U) \rtimes_\sigma \mathbb{R}$ to $C^*(U, \mathcal{F})$ in §5. Here we just point out that $C^*(U, \mathcal{F})$ is CCR and there is a further decomposition which expresses $C^*(U, \mathcal{F})$ as an extension of two C*-algebras of continuous traces (2.6).

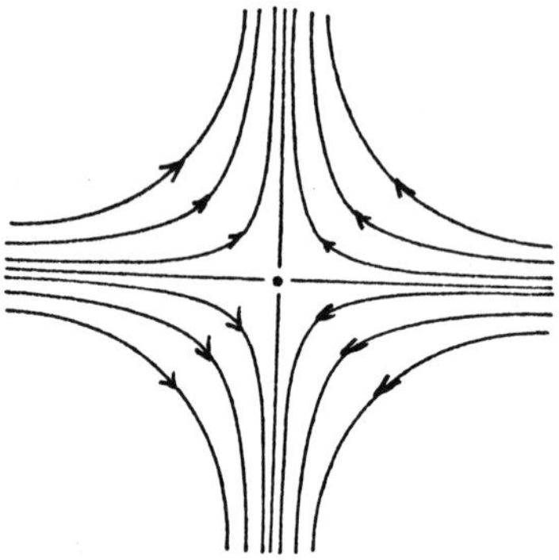

Figure 2.1

When p=1, q=1, the orbits of the $\mathbb{R}$-action on $\mathbb{R}^2$ are illustrated in Figure 2.1.

Let $X = \mathrm{span}(e_1,\ldots,e_p) \vee \mathrm{span}(e_{p+1},\ldots,e_{p+q}) \setminus \{0\} = \mathbb{R}^p \vee \mathbb{R}^q \setminus \{0\}$, i.e. the disjoint union of $\mathbb{R}^p$ and $\mathbb{R}^q$ with their common origin 0 deleted.

Let U_1 be the complement of X in U. Then U_1 is a saturated open submanifold of U.

By Proposition 1.4, we have an exact sequence for $C^*(U,\mathcal{F})$:

$$(2.6) \qquad 0 \to C^*(U_1,\mathcal{F}) \to C^*(U,\mathcal{F}) \xrightarrow{\pi'_X} C^*(X,\mathcal{F}) \to 0 \quad .$$

Now both the ideal and the quotient have very simple form. Observe first that the foliation on X arises from a submission of X onto a transversal $S^{p-1} \cup S^{q-1}$ because the $\mathbb{R}$-orbits in $\mathrm{span}(e_1,\ldots,e_p)$ and $\mathrm{span}(e_{p+1},\ldots,e_{p+q})$ are just the rays. Here "$\cup$" stands for disjoint union.

Note that the action of $\mathbb{R}$ on U, which is free with closed orbits, is *not* wandering, so Green's theorem does not apply ([Gr], Thm. 14). In particular, $C^*(U,\mathcal{G})$ is not a continuous trace C*-algebra. Recall that an action of a locally compact group G on a Hausdorff space X is *wandering* if the joint continuous map $G \times X \to X$ is proper.

By Proposition 1.2 (or [Gr], Thm. 14), there is a canonical isomorphism ψ_x:

$$C^*(X,\mathcal{G}) \xrightarrow[\psi_x]{} C(S^{p-1} \cup S^{q-1}, \mathcal{K}(L^2(\mathbb{R}))) \quad . \tag{2.7}$$

The foliation on U_1 also arises from a submersion. To visualize a transversal, fix any two points $P \in S^{p-1}$ and $Q \in S^{q-1}$. Form two open rays OP and OQ (see Figure 2.1). The interior of the quarter plane in $\mathbb{R}^{p+q}$ spanned by OP and OQ is in U_1. We denote it by $\mathring{S}_{PQ}$, which is homeomorphic to $\mathbb{R}^2$. Let $S_{PQ} = \overline{\mathring{S}_{PQ}} \setminus \{0\}$, the closed quarter plane with 0 deleted. The saturated open subset $\mathring{S}_{PQ}$ of S_{PQ} is foliated by hyperbolas and has the diagonal as a transversal. Letting $t > 0$ vary along this diagonal and letting P vary in S^{p-1} and Q vary in S^{q-1}, one obtains a transversal for U_1 which is a smooth suomanifold of U homeomorphic to $S^{p-1} \times S^{q-1} \times (0,\infty)$. The foliation on U_1 comes from this submersion and we have

$$C^*(U_1,\mathcal{G}) \cong C_0(S^{p-1} \times S^{q-1} \times (0,\infty)) \otimes \mathcal{K}(L^2(\mathbb{R})) \quad . \tag{2.8}$$

Now it is rather easy to see that $C^*(\hat{G}(p,q))$ as a set is homeomorphic to the union of $S^{p-1} \times S^{q-1} \times (0,\infty)$, S^{p-1}, S^{q-1} and a copy of $\mathbb{R}$. According to D. Williams [Wil], the topology on this set can be described as follows: the subspace topology on each component is just the usual Euclidean topology. For any nonempty subset E of S^{p-1} or S^{q-1}, the closure of A contains the entire line $\mathbb{R}$. Let $\Lambda = \{(x_n, y_n, t_n)\}$ be a sequence in $S^{p-1} \times S^{q-1} \times (0,\infty)$, $t_n \to 0$, then $\bar{\Lambda}$ contains the line $\mathbb{R}$ and any cluster points of $\{x_n\}$ in S^{p-1} and those of $\{y_n\}$ in S^{q-1}.

Since U_1 is also an open subset of $\mathbb{R}^{p+q}$, by Proposition 1.1 we have another short exact sequence for $C^*(G(p,q))^+$ in addition to (2.5):

$$(2.9) \qquad 0 \to C^*(U_1, \mathcal{G}) \to C^*(G(p,q))^+ \xrightarrow{\pi_X} B^+ \to 0$$

where

$$(2.10) \qquad B = C_0(\mathbb{R}^{p+q} \setminus U_1) \rtimes_\alpha \mathbb{R} = C_0(\mathbb{R}^p \vee \mathbb{R}^q) \rtimes_\alpha \mathbb{R} .$$

Finally, by applying Proposition 1.5 we have an exact sequence for B^+:

$$(2.11) \qquad 0 \to C^*(X, \mathcal{G}) \to B^+ \xrightarrow{\pi'_0} C(S^1) \to 0 .$$

We begin by studying the extension (2.11). We will be able to give an explicit description in this section. Recalling (2.7), we observe that (2.11) represents an element of the group

$$KK^1(C(S^1), C(S^{p-1} \cup S^{q-1})) \equiv Ext^1(C(S'), C(S^{p-1} \cup S^{q-1}))$$

The reader is referred to Kasparov [Kas 2] for the construction and basic facts about the KK-groups. These KK groups are very easy to compute by the universal coefficient theorem [R-S] because the related groups are torsion free and the C*-algebras are type I:

$$(2.12) \qquad KK^1(C(S^1), C(S^{p-1} \cup S^{q-1}))$$

$$\cong \mathrm{Hom}(K^1(S^1)), K^0(S^{p-1} \cup S^{q-1})) \oplus \mathrm{Hom}(K^0(S^1), K^0(S^{p-1} \cup S^{q-1}))$$

where of course $K^i(S^{p-1} \cup S^{q-1}) = K^i(S^{p-1}) \oplus K^i(S^{q-1})$.

The element in $KK^1(C(S^1), C(S^{p-1} \cup S^{q-1}))$ represented by B^+ is given by the connecting homomorphisms (δ_0, δ_1) in the six-term exact sequence [Ros & Sch]:

$$\text{(2.13)}\qquad \begin{array}{ccccc} K_0(C(S^{p-1} \cup S^{q-1}), \mathcal{K})) & \longrightarrow & K_0(B^+) & \longrightarrow & K_0(C(S^1)) \\ \delta_1 \uparrow & & & & \downarrow \delta_0 \\ K_1(C(S^1) & \longleftarrow & K_1(B^+) & \longleftarrow & K_1(C(S^{p-1} \cup S^{q-1}), \mathcal{K}) \end{array}$$

The extension (2.11) is uniquely determined by the Busby invariant [Bus]

$$\gamma \colon C(S^1) \longrightarrow M(C(S^{p-1} \cup S^{q-1}, \mathcal{K})) / C(S^{p-1} \cup S^{q-1}, \mathcal{K}) .$$

Note that $M(C(S^{p-1} \cup S^{q-1}, \mathcal{K}))$ is just $C_{S-*}(S^{p-1} \cup S^{q-1}, \mathcal{L}(H))$ according to [Ake], Corollaries 3.4 and 3.5. The preimage under the quotient $C_{*-S}(S^{p-1} \cup S^{q-1}, \mathcal{L}(H)) \to C_{*-S}(S^{p-1} \cup S^{q-1}), \mathcal{L}(H))/C(S^{p-1} \cup S^{q-1}, \mathcal{K})$ of Rang(γ) is a subalgebra of $C_{*-S}(S^{p-1} \cup S^{q-1}, \mathcal{L}(H))$ naturally isomorphic to B^+.

To specify the natural imbedding $\mu \colon B^+ \hookrightarrow C_{*-S}(S^{p-1} \cup S^{q-1}, \mathcal{L}(L^2(\mathbb{R}))$ recall the representation of $C^*(G)$ with supports on the $\mathbb{R}$-orbits represented by 0 and points in $S^{p-1} \cup S^{q-1}$.

We identify $L^1(\mathbb{R}^{p+q+1})$ with $L^1(G(p,q))$, which is densely contained in $C^*(G(p,q))$. Let $g \in L^1(\mathbb{R}^{p+q+1})$. For $\lambda \in \mathbb{R}$, the one-dimensional representation is

$$\text{(2.14)}\qquad \pi_\lambda(g) = \int_{\mathbb{R}^{p+q+1}} g(x,y,t)\, e^{it\lambda}\, dxdydt = \hat{g}(0,0,\lambda)$$

where $x \in \mathbb{R}^p$ and $y \in \mathbb{R}^q$. As usual $\hat{g}$ stands for the Fourier transformation of g.

For each $\zeta \in S^{q-1}$ there is an infinite dimensional irreducible representation given by

$$(2.15)\qquad (\pi_\zeta(g)f)(s) = \int_{\mathbb{R}^{p+q+1}} g(x,t,y)\ \langle y, e^{-S}\rho\rangle\ f(S-t)\,dxdydt$$

for $f \in L^2(\mathbb{R})$. For each $\eta \in S^{p-1}$ we have the same formula except a sign difference representing the reversed $\mathbb{R}$-action,

$$(2.16)\qquad (\pi_\eta(g)f)(s) = \int_{\mathbb{R}^{p+q+1}} g(x,y,t)\ \langle x, e^{s}\eta\rangle\ f(s-t)\,dxdydt \quad .$$

LEMMA 2.2. *The homomorphism* μ *of* $C^*(G(p,q))^+$ *into* $C_{*-S}(S^{p-1} \cup S^{q-1}, B(H))$ *defined by mapping* g *to* $(\rho \to \pi_\zeta(g))_{\zeta \in S^{p-1} \cup S^{q-1}}$ *has kernel isomorphic to* $C^*(U_1, \mathcal{G})$.

Proof. We only need notice that every one-dimensional representation given by $\lambda \in \mathbb{R}$ in (2.12) is weakly contained in $S^{p-1} \cup S^{q-1}$ in $\widehat{C^*(G)}$. The rest is clear. Q.E.D.

Let $\bar{\mu}$ be μ modulo its kernel. Then $\bar{\mu}$ is an imbedding of B^+ into $C_{*-S}(S^{p-1} \cup S^{q-1}, \mathcal{L}(H))$. It turns out that B^+ inherits some nice properties [R1] from its two building blocks.

LEMMA 2.3. (a) *The homomorphism* $\bar{\mu}$ *is a natural imbedding of* B^+ *into* $C(S^{p-1} \cup S^{q-1}, \mathcal{L}(H))$. *Hence the Busby invariant* γ *maps* $C(S^1)$ *into* $C(S^{p-1} \cup S^{q-1}, \mathcal{L}(H)/\mathcal{K})$.

(b) *For each* $f \in C(S^1)$, $\gamma(f)(\zeta)$ *is independent of* $\zeta \in S^{q-1}$. *The same is true for* $\zeta \in S^{p-1}$.

<u>Proof</u>. Observe that S^{p-1} and S^{q-1} are disjoint to both open and closed subsets of $S^{p-1} \cup S^{q-1}$. Part (a) follows immediately from Rosenberg's Property 3. Part (b) follows from a similar argument of Rosenberg's Property 4 [R1]. Since later we are going to show the stronger fact that $\gamma(f)(\zeta) = \gamma(f)(\eta)^*$ for any $\zeta \in S^{p-1}$, $\eta \in S^{q-1}$ and $f \in C(S^1)$, we don't repeat that discussion here. Q.E.D.

From now on we identify B^+ with the image of its imbedding in $C(S^{p-1} \cup S^{q-1}, \mathcal{L}(H))$.

For $K_1(C(S^1))$, we fix a generator $[z]$ where z is the identity function on S^1. For

$$K_0(C(S^r) \otimes \mathcal{K}(L^2(\mathbb{R}))) \simeq \begin{cases} \mathbb{Z}^2 & r \geq 0 \quad \text{even} \\ \mathbb{Z} & r \geq 1 \quad \text{odd} \end{cases}$$

we fix the basis as follows:

If $r = 0$, the two generators are $[p_1 \otimes q]$ and $[p_2 \otimes q]$, where p_1, p_2 are the characteristic functions of the two points of S^0, and q is a rank-1 projection in $\mathcal{L}(L^2(\mathbb{R}))$.

Now let $r > 0$. The first generator is of form $[1 \otimes q]$, where 1 is the constant on S^r. If r is even we fix the second generator to be any generator of $K_0(C_0(\mathbb{R}^r, \mathcal{K}(L^2(\mathbb{R})))$ which is contained in $K_0(C(S^r, \mathcal{K}(L^2(\mathbb{R}))))$. For instance, we may let the second generator be the Bott element $[b'] = [p \otimes q] - [1 \otimes q]$ where $[p]-[1]$ is the Bott element for $K_0(C(S^2))$ ([T], 8.5), and use periodicity to obtain the second generator for $r = 4, 6, \ldots$.

PROPOSITION 2.4. *In the group (see* (2.12)*)*

$$\text{Ext}(C(S^1),\ C(S^{p-1} \cup S^{q-1}, \mathcal{K})) \tag{2.17}$$

$$\approx \text{Hom}(K_0(C(S^1)),\ K_1(C(S^{p-1} \cup S^{q-1}, \mathcal{K})))$$

$$\oplus\ \text{Hom}(K_1(C(S^1)),\ K_0(C(S^{p-1} \cup S^{q-1}, \mathcal{K}))) \quad ,$$

the elements (δ_0, δ_1) *represented by the extension* (2.11) *are given as follows:*

(1) *The exponential map* δ_0 *is always zero.*

(2) *Fix the basis defined in the preceding paragraph for the second summand of* (2.17) *which decomposes as*

$$\text{Hom}(K_1(C(S^1)),\ K_0(C(S^{p-1}, \mathcal{K}))) \oplus \text{Hom}(K_1(C(S^1)),\ K_0(C(S^{q-1}, \mathcal{K}))) \quad .$$

Then the index map δ_1 *gives the following elements in* $\text{Hom}(K_1(C(S^1),\ K_0(C(S^{q-1}, \mathcal{K}))):$

$$\begin{cases} (-1,\ -1) \in \mathbb{Z}^2 & \text{if} \quad q = 1 \\ \quad -1 \in \mathbb{Z} & \text{if} \quad q = \text{even} \\ (-1,\ 0) \in \mathbb{Z}^2 & \text{if} \quad q = \text{odd and } >1 \quad . \end{cases} \tag{2.18}$$

The elements given by δ_1 *in* $\text{Hom}(K_1(C(S^1)),\ K_0(C(S^{p-1}, \mathcal{K})))$ *are the same except the signs are all reversed.*

<u>Proof</u>. (1) Recall that the exact sequence (2.11) is just the unitalization of the following exact sequence:

$$0 \longrightarrow C^*(X, \mathcal{G}) \longrightarrow B \longrightarrow C_0(\mathbb{R}) \longrightarrow 0 \quad . \tag{2.19}$$

Since $K_0(C_0(\mathbb{R})) = 0$, the exponential map in the six-term exact sequence of (2.19) is zero. Since $K_0(C(S^1))$ is generated by the identity whose preimage in B^+ can also be chosen to be the identity, the image of δ_0 in $\mathrm{Hom}(K_0(C(S^1)), K_1(C(S^{p-1} \cup S^{q-1}, \mathcal{K})))$ is just the zero element.

(2) Claim that the image of $\delta_1[z]$ of the generator z of $K_1(C(S^1))$ under the index map δ_1 makes no contribution to the subgroup $K_0(C_0(\mathbb{R}^{q-1}, \mathcal{K})) \subset K_0(C(S^{q-1}, \mathcal{K}))$. To see this, let u be a preimage in $M_2(B^+)$ of $z \oplus \bar{z}$ (cf. (2.7) and (2.11)). By Lemma 2.3, $u \in C(S^{p-1} \cup S^{q-1}, M_2(B(H)))$ and $u(\zeta) \bmod (M_2(\mathcal{K}))$ $(u(\eta) \bmod (M_2(\mathcal{K}))$ is independent of $\zeta \in S^{p-1}$ $(\eta \in S^{q-1})$. Fix $u_0 = u(\zeta_0)$ $(u_1 = u(\eta_1))$ for some $\zeta_0 \in S^{p-1}$ $(\eta_1 \in S^{q-1}$. Let $v \in C(S^{p-1} \cup S^{q-1}, M_2(\mathcal{L}(H)))$, taking constant value u_0 on S^{p-1} and u_1 on S^{q-1}. Then $(u-v) \bmod (M_2(\mathcal{K})) = 0$ and $u-v \in C(S^{p-1} \cup S^{q-1}, M_2(\mathcal{K})) \subset M_2(B^+)$. Thus $v = (v-u)+u \in M_2(B^+)$ and is still a preimage of $z \oplus \bar{z}$. Hence the $K_0(C(S^{p-1}, \mathcal{K}))$-component of $\delta_1([z])$ is contained in the subgroup of $K_0(C(S^{p-1}, \mathcal{K}))$ generated by the element $[1 \otimes q]$.

We verify now that for each connected component S_C^{p-1} of S^{p-1}, the $K_0(C(S_C^{p-1}, \mathcal{K}))$-component of $\delta_1[z]$ is precisely the negative trivial generator of $K_0(C(S_C^{p-1}, \mathcal{K}))$. The proof again can be modeled after that of ([R1], Prop. 5). We define $g \in L^1(\mathbb{R}^{p+q+1}) \subset C^*(G(p,q))$ by

(2.20) $$g(x,y,t) = -2h(x,y)\, \chi_{[0,\infty)}(t) e^{-t}$$

for $X \in \mathbb{R}^p$, $y \in \mathbb{R}^q$, $t \in \mathbb{R}$. Here $h \in L^1(\mathbb{R}^{p+q})$ and the Fourier transform $\hat{h}(x,y)$ is a function depending only on x^2+y^2, with $\hat{h}(0,0) = 1$. One easily verifies that ([R1], p.186)

(2.21) $$1+\pi_0(g):\ t \longmapsto \frac{it+1}{it-1}\ , \qquad t \in \mathbb{R}\ ,$$

(see (2.5)). So $1+\pi_0(g) = z$ in $C(S^1)$ if $\mathbb{R}^+$ is identified with S^1 by the usual homeomorphism (2.21). Thus a preimage of z (see (2.11)) is given by

$$(2.22) \qquad 1+\pi_x(g):\ S^{p-1} \cup S^{q-1} \longrightarrow B(H) \quad ,$$
$$\longrightarrow \pi_\zeta(g) \quad .$$

Now by a computation which is completely analogous to that in the proof of Proposition 5 [R1], one sees that the Fredholm index of $[1+\pi_x(g)](\rho)$ is -1. This is true for all $\rho \in S^{q-1}$.

For $\eta \in S^{q-1}$ we can check that the Fredholm index of $[1+\pi_x(g)](\eta)$ is 1. The difference in sign is due to the reversed direction of the $\mathbb{R}$-action.

Q.E.D.

Now let's give an explicit description of the structure of B^+.

THEOREM 2.5. *Assume the notation in Theorem 2.1. Let* B *be* $C_0(\mathbb{R}^p \vee \mathbb{R}^q) \rtimes_\alpha \mathbb{R}$ *as in* (2.10). *There is a natural isomorphism* ψ *such that*

$$(2.23) \qquad B^+ \cong \{f \in C(S^{p-1} \cup S^{q-1}, C^*(S)) \mid \pi(f(x) = \overline{\pi(f(y))} \in C(S^1) \text{ for all } x \in S^{p-1},\ y \in S^{q-1}\} \quad .$$

Let $\bar{B}$ *be the* C^**-algebra on the right-hand side of* (2.23). *Then*

$$(2.24) \qquad \begin{array}{ccccccccc} 0 & \longrightarrow & C^*(X,\mathcal{G}) & \longrightarrow & B^+ & \longrightarrow & C(S^1) & \longrightarrow & 0 \\ & & \cong \downarrow \psi_x & & \cong \downarrow \psi & & \| & & \\ 0 & \longrightarrow & C(S^{p-1} \cup S^{q-1}, \mathcal{K}) & \longrightarrow & \bar{B} & \longrightarrow & C(S^1) & \longrightarrow & 0 \\ & & & & f & \longmapsto & \pi(f(x)) & & \end{array}$$

commutes (cf. (2.7)*).*

<u>Proof</u>. We use a combination of techniques used by Green ([Gr],

Lemma 6) and Rosenberg ([R1], Prop. 5). Define a function $g_0 \in L^1(\mathbb{R}^{p+q+1}) \subset C^*(G(p,q))$ by

$$g_0(x,y,t) = -h(x,y)\,\chi_{[0,\infty)}(t)\,e^{-t/2} \tag{2.25}$$

for $x \in \mathbb{R}^p$, $y \in \mathbb{R}^q$ and $t \in \mathbb{R}$, where we choose $h \in C_0(\mathbb{R}^{p+q}) \cap L^1(\mathbb{R}^{p+q})$ satisfying the following properties:

i) The Fourier transform $\hat{h}(x,y)$ depends only on the distance of (x,y) to the origin.

ii) $0 \leq \hat{h}(x,y) \leq 1$ for all $(x,y) \in \mathbb{R}^{p+q}$.

iii) $\hat{h}(x,y) = 1$ for $|(x,y)| < \delta_0$ and $\hat{h}(x,y) = 0$ for $|(x,y)| > N_0$ where $N_0 > \delta_0 > 1$ are constants.

To see that such h exists, take a function h_0 in $C_c(\mathbb{R}^{p+q})$ such that (i), (ii) and (iii) are satisfied and its inverse Fourier transform h is in L^1. Since h_0 is contained in $L^1(\mathbb{R}^{p+q}) \cap L^2(\mathbb{R}^{p+q})$, we have $h_0 = \hat{h}$. For $\lambda \in \mathbb{R}$, (2.14) gives

$$\begin{aligned} \pi_\lambda(g_0) &= \int_{\mathbb{R}^{p+q+1}} g_0(x,y,t)\,e^{it\lambda}\,dxdydt \\ &= -\hat{h}(0,0)\int_{-\infty}^{\infty} e^{t(i\lambda - \frac{1}{2})}\,dt = \frac{1}{i\lambda - \frac{1}{2}} . \end{aligned}$$

Denote $\theta = (\lambda \to 1 + \pi_\lambda(g_0))$, $\theta \in C_0(\mathbb{R})^+ \cong C(S^1)$,

$$\theta(\lambda) = \frac{i\lambda + \frac{1}{2}}{i\lambda - \frac{1}{2}} . \tag{2.26}$$

The polynomials in θ and $\bar{\theta}$ are dense in $C_0(\mathbb{R})^+ \simeq C(S^1)$ by the Stone-Weierstrass theorem.

The continuous cross section given by g_0 over $S^{p-1} \cup S^{q-1} \subset C^*(G(p,q))^\wedge$ specifies a preimage of θ in B^+ (see (2.9)). Let $\zeta \in S^{q-1}$, $\eta \in S^{p-1}$.

Recall (2.13); for $f \in L^2(\mathbb{R})$ we have

$$(\pi_\zeta(g_0)f)(s) = \int_{\mathbb{R}^{p+q+1}} g_0(x,y,t)\exp(ie^{-s}\langle y,\zeta\rangle_{\mathbb{R}^p})f(s-t)\,dxdydt$$

$$= \int_{\mathbb{R}} \tilde{g}_0(e^{-s}\zeta, 0, t)f(s-t)\,dt$$

$$= -\hat{h}(e^{-s}\zeta, 0)\int_0^\infty e^{-t/2} f(s-t)\,dt$$

where $\tilde{g}_0$ stands for the Fourier transform of g_0 in its first p+q variables.

Define $T \in \mathcal{L}(L^2(\mathbb{R}))$ by

(2.27) $$(Tf)(s) = -\chi_{[0,\infty)}(s)\int_0^\infty e^{-t/2} f(s-t)\,dt \quad .$$

Then T is a compact perturbation of $\pi_\zeta(g_0)$ because the integral operator $(\pi_\zeta(g_0) - T)$ has a square integrable kernel function and thus is a Hilbert-Schmidt operator. Notice that T is independent of $\zeta \in S^{p-1}$. Now $L^2(\mathbb{R})$ is the direct sum of $L^2(-\infty,0)$ and $L^2(0,\infty)$. For $L^2(0,\infty)$ we fix an orthonormal basis $\{e_n\}_{n=0,1,2,...}$,

(2.28) $$e_n(t) = L_n(t)\, e^{-t/2} \quad , \quad t \geq 0$$

where $L_n(t) = \sum_{i=0}^{n} \binom{n}{i} \frac{(-t)^i}{i!}$ are the Laguerre polynomials,

For $L^2(-\infty,0)$ we fix an orthonormal basis $\{f_n\}_{n=0,1,...}$, "symmetric" to $\{e_n\}$,

(2.29) $$f_n(t) = -L_n(-t)\, e^{t/2} \quad , \quad t \leq 0 \quad .$$

We consider e_n, f_n as elements of $L^2(\mathbb{R})$ by letting them take value 0 on the other half of the line. Then $\{e_n, f_n\}_{n=0,1,2,\ldots}$ forms a basis for $L^2(\mathbb{R})$.

For $s > 0$,

$$(Tf)(s) = -\int_0^\infty e^{-t/2} f(s-t)dt \quad .$$

If $\operatorname{supp}(f) \subset (-\infty, 0]$, then

$$(Tf)(s) = -\int_s^\infty e^{-t/2} f(s-t)dt$$

$$= -e^{-s/2} \int_{-\infty}^0 e^{-t/2} f(t)dt$$

hence for $s > 0$, $$Tf_n(s) = \begin{cases} 0 & n=1,2,\ldots \\ e^{-s/2} = e_0(s) & n=0 \quad . \end{cases}$$

For $s < 0$, $(Tf)(s) = 0$. Thus

$$(1+T)f_n = \begin{cases} f_n & n=1,2,\ldots \\ f_0 + e_0 & n=0 \quad . \end{cases} \tag{2.30}$$

The following calculation shows that (1+T) acts on $\{e_n\}$ as the unilateral shift. For $s > 0$,

$$(1+T)e_n(s) = e_n(s) - \int_0^\infty e^{-t/2} e_n(s-t)dt$$

$$= e^{-s/2} L_n(s) - \int_0^s e^{-t/2} e^{-(s-t)/2} L_n(s-t)dt$$

$$= e^{-s/2}(L_n(s) - \int_0^s L_n(s-t)dt)$$

$$= e^{-s/2}(L_n(s) - \int_0^s L_n(t)dt) = e^{-s/2} L_{n+1}(s)$$

$$= e_{n+1}(s) \quad .$$

Here we have used an identity for Laguerre polynomials

$$L_{n+1}(s) = L_n(s) - \int_0^s L_n(t)dt \quad . \tag{2.31}$$

For $s<0$, $((1+T)e_n)(s) = e_n(s) = 0$. Therefore,

$$(1+T)e_n = e_{n+1} \quad , \qquad n=0,1,2,\ldots \quad . \tag{2.32}$$

Hence up to a rank-1 operator $(1+T)$ is just $id_{L^2(-\infty,0)} \oplus S_{L^2(0,\infty)}$.

Assume now that $\eta \in S^{q-1}$. We study the action of $\pi_\eta(g_0)$ on $L^2(\mathbb{R})$ which corresponds to the orbit of η. Again by (2.16),

$$\begin{aligned}\pi_\eta(g_0)f(s) &= \int_{\mathbb{R}^{p+q+1}} g_0(x,y,t)\exp(ie\langle y,\eta\rangle)f(s-t)dxdydt \\ &= \int_{\mathbb{R}} \tilde{g}_0(0,\ e^s\eta,\ t)f(s-t)dt \\ &= -\hat{h}(0,e^s)\int_0^\infty f(s-t)e^{-t/2}\,dt \quad .\end{aligned}$$

This time we let $T' \in B(L^2(\mathbb{R}))$ be given by

$$T'f(s) = -\chi_{(-\infty,0]}(s)\int_0^\infty f(s-t)e^{-t/2}\,dt \quad . \tag{2.33}$$

Then again $(T' - \pi_\eta(g)) \in K(L^2(\mathbb{R}))$. For $s<0$,

$$T'f(s) = -\int_0^\infty f(s-t)e^{-t/2}\,dt \quad .$$

If $\operatorname{supp}(f) \subset (0,\infty)$, then for $s<0$, $T'f(s) = 0$. For $s>0$, $T'f(s) = 0$. Thus $T'e_n = 0$ and

$$(1+T')e_n = e_n \quad , \qquad n=0,1,2,\ldots \quad . \tag{2.34}$$

Notice that f_n has support in $(-\infty,0]$. Then for $s<0$,

$$(1+T')f_n(s) = f_n(s) - \int_0^\infty e^{-t/2} f_n(s-t)dt$$

$$= e^{s/2}(-L_n(-s) + \int_0^\infty e^{-t} L_n(t-s)dt) .$$

If n=0, $L_0(t) = 1$ and

$$(1+T')f_0(s) = e^{s/2}(-1 + \int_0^\infty e^{-t} dt) = 0 .$$

If n>0, then

$$\int_0^\infty e^{-t/2}(L_n(t)e^{-t/2})dt = 0$$

so for $s < 0$,

$$(1+T')f_n(s) = e^{s/2}(-L_n(-s) + e^{-s} \int_{-s}^\infty e^{-t} L_n(t)dt$$

$$= e^{s/2}(-L_n(-s) - e^{-s} \int_0^{-s} e^{-t} L_n(t)dt$$

$$= e^{s/2} L_{n-1}(-s) = f_{n-1}(s) .$$

To see above that

$$(2.35) \qquad L_n(s) + e^s \int_0^s e^{-t} L_n(t)dt = L_{n-1}(s) , \qquad s > 0,$$

multiply both sides by e^{-s}, differentiate and simplify, to get

$$L_n'(s) = L_{n-1}'(s) - L_{n-1}(s)$$

which is true by identity (2.31). Since (2.35) holds for s=0, it holds for all s as both sides have the same derivatives.

For $s > 0$, $T'f_n(s) = 0$, $(1+T')f_n(s) = f_n(s) = 0$, $n=0,1,\ldots,$ therefore

$$(2.36) \qquad \begin{cases} (1+T')f_n = f_{n-1} & n=1,2,3,\ldots \\ (1+T')f_0 = 0 . \end{cases}$$

Summarizing (2.34) and (2.36) we see that $(1+T')$ acts as

$S^{*}_{L^2(-\infty,0)} \oplus \mathrm{id}_{L^2(0,\infty)}$ on $L^2(\mathbb{R})$,

Define $S_1 \in C(S^{p-1} \cup S^{q-1}, B(L^2(\mathbb{R})))$ by

(2.37)
$$\begin{aligned} S_1(\zeta) &= \mathrm{id}_{L^2(-\infty,0)} \oplus S_{L^2(0,\infty)} && \text{for} \quad \zeta \in S^{p-1} \\ S_1(\eta) &= S^{*}_{L^2(-\infty,0)} \oplus \mathrm{id}_{L^2(0,\infty)} && \text{for} \quad \eta \in S^{q-1} . \end{aligned}$$

Then from the discussion above,

(2.38)
$$(S_1 - (I + \pi_x(g_0))) \in C(S^{p-1} \cup S^{q-1}, \mathcal{K}(L^2(\mathbb{R})))$$

where π_x is the quotient map in (2.9).

From (2.11), $C(S^{p-1} \cup S^{q-1}, \mathcal{K}(L^2(\mathbb{R}))$ is an ideal of $B^+ \subset C(S^{p-1} \cup S^{q-1}, B(L^2(\mathbb{R})))$. Thus $\pi_x(g_0) \in B^+$ implies that $S_1 \in B^+$. Also (2.38) implies the fact that under the quotient map $\pi_0 \colon B^+ \to C_0(\mathbb{R})^+$ (see (2.11)), S_1 and $(I + \pi_x(g_0))$ have the same image. We already know that π_0 maps $(I + \pi_x(g_0))$ to θ, so $\pi_0(S_1) = \theta$ and $\pi_0(S_1^*) = \bar{\theta}$.

Let $C^*(S_1)$ be the C^*-algebra generated by S_1, S_1^*, and the ideal $C(S^{p-1} \cup S^{q-1}, \mathcal{K})$. Then $C^*(S_1) \subset B^+$. Since the polynomials in θ and $\bar{\theta}$ are dense in $C_0(\mathbb{R})^+$, the restriction of π_0 on $C^*(S_1)$ is onto. We have the following commuting diagram

(2.38)
$$\begin{array}{ccccccccc} 0 & \longrightarrow & C(S^{p-1} \cup S^{q-1}, \mathcal{K}) & \longrightarrow & C^*(S_1) & \longrightarrow & C_0(\mathbb{R})^+ & \longrightarrow & 0 \\ & & \| & & \downarrow & S_1 \longrightarrow \theta & \| & & \\ & & \| & & \downarrow & \downarrow & \| & & \\ & & \| & & \downarrow & S_1 \longrightarrow \theta & \| & & \\ 0 & \longrightarrow & C(S^{p-1} \cup S^{q-1}, \mathcal{K}) & \longrightarrow & B^+ & \xrightarrow{\pi_0} & C_0(\mathbb{R})^+ & \longrightarrow & 0 \end{array}$$

By the Five Lemma, or by a direct diagram chasing, we see that the middle inclusion is actually onto.

Finally we observe that

$$C^*(S_1) \cong \{f \in C(S^{p-1} \cup S^{q-1}, C^*(S \oplus \mathrm{id})) \mid \pi'(f(\zeta)) = \overline{\pi'(f(\eta))} \text{ for all } \zeta \in S^{p-1},\ \eta \in S^{q-1}\}, \tag{2.39}$$

where as usual $C^*(S \oplus \mathrm{id})$ stands for the C*-algebra generated by $S \oplus \mathrm{id}$, $S^* \oplus \mathrm{id}$, and $\mathcal{K}(H \oplus H)$, π' is the quotient homomorphism from $C^*(S \oplus \mathrm{id})$ to $C(S^1)$ taking $S \oplus \mathrm{id}$ to z. By BDF theory we know that $S \oplus \mathrm{id}$ and S are unitarily equivalent modulo compact operators and $C^*(S \oplus \mathrm{id})$ and $C^*(S)$ are isomorphic as extensions of $\mathcal{K}$ by $C(S^1)$ (See [D], Thm. 2, p.9), i.e.

$$\begin{array}{ccccccccc} 0 & \longrightarrow & \mathcal{K}(H \oplus H) & \longrightarrow & C^*(S \oplus \mathrm{id}) & \longrightarrow & C(S^1) & \longrightarrow & 0 \\ & & \downarrow \simeq & & \phi_0 \downarrow \simeq & & \| & & \\ 0 & \longrightarrow & \mathcal{K}(H) & \longrightarrow & C^*(S) & \longrightarrow & C(S^1) & \longrightarrow & 0 \end{array} \tag{2.38'}$$

Hence we have the following commuting diagram

$$\begin{array}{ccccccccc} 0 & \longrightarrow & C(S^{p-1} \cup S^{q-1}, \mathcal{K}) & \longrightarrow & \overline{B} & \longrightarrow & C(S^1) & \longrightarrow & 0 \\ & & \uparrow \simeq & & \alpha \uparrow \simeq & & \| & & \\ 0 & \longrightarrow & C(S^{p-1} \cup S^{q-1}, \mathcal{K}) & \longrightarrow & C(S_1) & \longrightarrow & C(S^1) & \longrightarrow & 0 \\ & & \| & & \| & & \beta \uparrow \simeq & & \\ 0 & \longrightarrow & C(S^{p-1} \cup S^{q-1}, \mathcal{K}) & \longrightarrow & B^+ & \longrightarrow & C_0(\mathbb{R})^+ & \longrightarrow & 0 \end{array} \tag{2.40}$$

where the isomorphisms α and β are as follows: $\alpha(S_1)$ is the function taking constant value S (S^*) on S^{p-1} (S^{q-1}), $\beta(\theta) = z$. The quotient map γ takes S_1 to z. Clearly (2.23) and (2.24) follow from (2.40).

Q.E.D.

Example. (a) Let G_0 be the proper "ax+b" group, i.e. the proper affine group of the reals $G_0 = \{(a,b) : a > 0,\ b \in \mathbb{R}\}$ with the multiplication rule $(a_1,b_1)(a_2,b_2) = (a_1a_2,\ a_1b_2 + b_1)$. From the proof of Theorem 2.5,

$$C^*(G_0) \simeq \{(\alpha,\beta) \in C^*(\mathrm{id} \oplus S)^2 \mid \pi'(\alpha) = \pi'(\beta) \in C(S^1)\}$$

$$\simeq \{(\alpha,\beta) \in C^*(S)^2 \mid \pi(\alpha) = \pi(\beta) \in C(S^1)\} \quad .$$

Cf. [Zep].

Figure 2.2

§3. $C^*(G(p,q))$ AS A CONTINUOUS FIELD OF C*-ALGEBRAS

A natural approach for analyzing the structure of a given C*-algebra is to decompose it as a field of C*-algebras over its spectrum. With our preparation from previous sections, we can extract a certain amount of information about $C^*(G(p,q))$ by this approach. This will give us a good overview before we go deeper, in the next section, by exploiting the ideas coming from foliations.

We determined the spectrum $C^*(G(p,q))^\wedge$ in §2. Recall that the "generic" leaf space of the foliation, which we identified with

$S^{p-1} \times S^{q-1} \times (0,\infty)$, is a dense open subset of $C^*(G(p,q))^\wedge$. Thus we are going to write $C^*(G(p,q))^+$ and its various ideals as continuous fields of C*-algebras over this subset.

By the "Mackey machine" on every point $P = (\gamma\zeta, \gamma'\eta) \in \hat{\mathbb{R}}^{p+q} \setminus \{0\}$ ($\gamma, \gamma' > 0$, $\zeta \in S^{p-1}$, $\eta \in S^{q-1}$) lives an infinite dimensional irreducible representation of $G(p,q)$ given by

$$\pi_P(x,y,t)f(s) = \exp i(\gamma e^{-s}\langle x,\zeta\rangle_{\mathbb{R}^p} + \gamma' e^{s}\langle y,\eta\rangle_{\mathbb{R}^q}) \cdot f(s-t)$$

where $(x,y,t) \in G(p,q)$, $f \in L^2(\mathbb{R})$.

For $g \in L^1(\mathbb{R}^{p+q+1}) \subset C^*(G(p,q))$, the corresponding representation is given by the integrated form, still denoted by π_P:

$$(3.1) \qquad \pi_P(g)f(s) = \int_{\mathbb{R}^{p+q+1}} g(x,y,t)\exp i(\gamma e^{-s}\langle x,\zeta\rangle_{\mathbb{R}^p} + \gamma' e^{s}\langle y,\eta\rangle_{\mathbb{R}^q}) \cdot f(s-t)\,dxdydt$$

$$= \int_{\mathbb{R}} \tilde{g}(\gamma e^{-s}\zeta, \gamma' e^{s}\eta, t)f(s-t)dt \ .$$

As before $\tilde{g}$ denotes the Fourier transform of g in its first $p+q$ variables.

In the preceding section we found that for every $P \in \mathbb{R}^p \vee \mathbb{R}^q \setminus \{0\}$, $\pi_P(g)$ is noncompact in general for $g \in C^*(G(p,q))$. However for a "generic" irreducible representation π_P, $P \in \mathbb{R}^{p+q} \setminus (\mathbb{R}^p \vee \mathbb{R}^q)$, $\pi_P(g)$ turns out to be a compact operator for all $g \in C^*(G(p,q))$.

LEMMA 3.1. *For every* $g \in C^*(G(p,q))$, *the mapping sending* P *to* $\pi_P(g)$ *is a norm continuous map from* $\mathbb{R}^{p+q} \setminus (\mathbb{R}^p \vee \mathbb{R}^q)$ *into* $\mathcal{K}(L^2(\mathbb{R}))$. *Moreover,* $\|\pi_P(g)\| \to 0$ *as* $P \to \infty$.

Proof. We first remark that once we have shown that for any element g in a dense subalgebra of $C^*(G(p,q))$, the mapping $P \longrightarrow \pi_P(g)$ is continuous in norm and $\|\pi_P(g)\| \to 0$ as $P \to \infty$, then by the standard triangle-inequality argument those will be true for any $g_1 \in C^*(G(p,q))$. Here we need the fact that $\|g - g_1\| \geq \|\pi_P(g) - \pi_P(g_1)\|$ for all P. This simple remark will be used repeatedly in this paper to simplify our estimates, without further mention.

Since $C_c(\hat{\mathbb{R}}^{p+q})$ is dense in $C_0(\hat{\mathbb{R}}^{p+q}) \approx C^*(\mathbb{R}^{p+q})$, so $C_c(\hat{\mathbb{R}}, C_c(\mathbb{R}^{p+q}))$ is dense in $C^*(G(p,q))$. Now fix any $g \in C^*(G(p,q))$ such that $\tilde{g} \in C_c(\hat{\mathbb{R}}^{p+q} \times \mathbb{R})$. Assume $\operatorname{supp}(\tilde{g}) \subset B_0(N)$, the open ball of radius N centered at 0, for some $N > 0$. Let $P_i = (\gamma_i\zeta_i, \gamma_i'\eta_i) \in \mathbb{R}^{p+q} \setminus (\mathbb{R}^p \vee \mathbb{R}^q)$, $i=1,2$. We show that

$$\|\pi_{P_1}(g) - \pi_{P_2}(g)\| \longrightarrow 0 \quad \text{as} \quad P_2 \longrightarrow P_1 \ . \tag{3.2}$$

A routine computation yields

$$\begin{aligned} &\|\pi_{P_1}(g)f - \pi_{P_2}(g)f\|_2^2 \\ &= \int_{\mathbb{R}} \left| \int_{\mathbb{R}} (\tilde{g}(\gamma_1 e^{-s}\zeta_1, \gamma_1' e^{s}\eta_1, t) - \tilde{g}(\gamma_2 e^{-s}\zeta_2, \gamma_2' e^{s}\eta_2, t)) f(s-t)dt \right|^2 ds \\ &= \int_{\mathbb{R}} \left| \int_{\mathbb{R}} (\tilde{g}(\gamma_1 e^{-s}\zeta_1, \gamma_1' e^{s}\eta_1, s-t) - \tilde{g}(\gamma_2 e^{-s}\zeta_2, \gamma_2' e^{s}\eta_2, s-t)) f(t)dt \right|^2 ds \\ &\leq \iint_{\mathbb{R}^2} \left| \tilde{g}(\gamma_1 e^{-s}\zeta_1, \gamma_1' e^{s}\eta_1, s-t) - \tilde{g}(\gamma_2 e^{-s}\zeta_2, \gamma_2' e^{s}\eta_2, s-t) \right|^2 dtds \, \|f\|_2^2 \ . \end{aligned} \tag{3.3}$$

Thus

$$\|\pi_{P_1}(g) - \pi_{P_2}(g)\|$$

$$\leq \iint_{\mathbb{R}} \left|\tilde{g}(\gamma_1 e^{-s}\zeta_1, \gamma_1' e^{s}\eta_1, s-t) - \tilde{g}(\gamma_2 e^{-s}\zeta_2, \gamma_2' e^{s}\eta_2, s-t)\right|^2 dtds$$

$$= \iint_{\mathbb{R}^2} \left|\tilde{g}(\gamma_1 e^{-s}\zeta_1, \gamma_1' e^{s}\zeta_1, t) - g(\gamma_2 e^{-s}\eta_2, \gamma_2' e^{s}\eta_2, t)\right|^2 dtds \quad .$$

Given $\varepsilon > 0$, there is $\delta > 0$ such that

$$|\tilde{g}(x_1) - \tilde{g}(x_2)| < \varepsilon \qquad \text{if } |x_1 - x_2| < \delta \tag{3.4}$$
$$x_1, x_2 \in \mathbb{R}^{p+q} \quad .$$

This can be done since $\tilde{g}$ is compactly supported.

For fixed P_1 we have

$$\tilde{g}(\gamma_1 e^{-s}\zeta_1, \gamma_1' e^{s}\eta_1, t) = 0 \quad \text{if} \quad s > \ell n \frac{N}{\gamma_1'} \quad \text{or} \quad s < -\ell n \frac{N}{\gamma_1} \quad \text{or} \quad |t| > N \quad . \tag{3.5}$$

When P_2 closes to P_1 enough so $\gamma_2 \geq \gamma_1/2$, $\gamma_2' > \gamma_1'/2$, then

$$\tilde{g}(\gamma_2 e^{-s}\zeta_1, \gamma_2' e^{s}\eta_1, t) = 0 \quad \text{if} \quad s > \ell n \frac{2N}{\gamma_1'} \quad \text{or} \quad s < -\ell n \frac{2N}{\gamma_1} \quad \text{or} \quad |t| > N \quad .$$

It follows from (3.3) that

$$\|\pi_{P_1}(g) - \pi_{P_2}(g)\|^2$$

$$= \int_{-\ell n \frac{2N}{\gamma_1}}^{\ell n \frac{2N}{\gamma'}} \int_{-N}^{N} \left|\tilde{g}(\gamma_1 e^{-s}\zeta_1, \gamma_1 e^{s}\eta_1, t) - \tilde{g}(\gamma_2 e^{-s}\zeta_2, \gamma_2' e^{s}\eta_2, t)\right|^2 dtds$$

$$\leq (\ell n \frac{2N}{\gamma'} + \ell n \frac{2N}{\gamma_1}) \cdot 2N \cdot \varepsilon$$

when $|\gamma_1 - \gamma_2| + |\gamma_1' - \gamma_2'| < \delta e^{-N}$. Thus (3.2) is true.

A similar estimate shows that for $P = (\gamma\zeta, \gamma'\eta) \in \hat{\mathbb{R}}^{p+q} \setminus (\hat{\mathbb{R}}^p \vee \hat{\mathbb{R}}^q)$ we have

$$(3.6) \qquad \|\pi_P(g)\|^2 \leq \iint |\tilde{g}(\gamma e^{-s}\zeta, \gamma' e^s\eta, t)|^2 \, dtds$$

$$= \int_{-\ln\frac{N}{\gamma'}}^{\ln\frac{N}{\gamma}} \int_{-N}^{N} |\tilde{g}(\gamma e^{-s}\zeta_1, \gamma' e^s\eta, t)|^2 \, dtds$$

$$= 0 \quad \text{when} \quad \gamma > N \quad \text{and} \quad \gamma' > N .$$

The above estimate also tells us that $\pi_P(g)$ is a Hilbert-Schmidt operator, in particular, a compact operator for every $P \in \hat{\mathbb{R}}^{p+q} \setminus (\hat{\mathbb{R}}^p \vee \hat{\mathbb{R}}^q)$.

For any $g \in C^*(G(p,q))$, choose a sequence $g_n \to g$, $g_n \in C_c(\mathbb{R}, C_c(\hat{\mathbb{R}}^{p+q}))$. Then

$$\|\pi_P(g_n) - \pi_P(g)\| < \|g_n - g\| \longrightarrow 0$$

so $\pi_P(g) \in \mathcal{K}(L^2(\mathbb{R}))$. Q.E.D.

Recall that π_P is unitarily equivalent to $\pi_{P'}$ iff P and P' are contained in the same leaf. For every $P \in \mathbb{R}^{p+q} \setminus \{\mathbb{R}^p \vee \mathbb{R}^q\}$ there is a unique $m = (\zeta,\eta,\gamma) \in S^{p-1} \times S^{q-1} \times (0,\infty)$ such that P and $(\gamma\zeta,\gamma\eta)$ are in the same leaf.

The natural mapping ψ: $g \mapsto (m \mapsto \pi_m(g))$ specifies a homomorphism of $C^*(G(p,q))$ into $C^b_{*-S}(S^{p-1} \times S^{q-1} \times (0,\infty), B(H))$. The homomorphism ψ expresses $C^*(G(p,q))$ as a field of C*-algebras over its "reduced spectrum". Since the weak closure of $S^{p-1} \times S^{q-1} \times (0,\infty)$ is all of

$C^*(G(p,q))^\wedge$, ψ is injective. We have proved

COROLLARY 3.2. *The natural homomorphism* ψ *embeds* $C^*(G(p,q))$ *into* $C^b(S^{p-1} \times S^{q-1} \times (0,\infty), K(L^2(\mathbb{R})))$. *Moreover, for every* $g \in C^*(G(p,q))$ *we have* $\|(\psi g)(m)\| \to 0$ *as* $m \to \infty$.

As we have shown in §3, $\pi_P(g)$ is no longer compact in general when $P \in \hat{\mathbb{R}}^p \vee \hat{\mathbb{R}}^q$. Therefore $\pi_P(g)$ may not converge in norm topology to a limit when P tends to a point in $\hat{\mathbb{R}}^p \vee \hat{\mathbb{R}}^q$ along a path in $\hat{\mathbb{R}}^{p+q} \setminus \{\hat{\mathbb{R}}^p \vee \hat{\mathbb{R}}^q\}$. Nevertheless we have

THEOREM 3.3. *The natural imbedding* $\psi: g \mapsto (m \mapsto \pi_m(g))$ *identifies* $C^*(G(p,q))^+$ *with a* C*-*subalgebra of* $C^b(S^{p-1} \times S^{q-1} \times (0,\infty), K(L^2(\mathbb{R})))$ *such that for every* $g \in C^*(G(p,q))^+$ *the following holds:*

i) $(\psi g)(m) \to \lambda_g I$ *in norm when* $m = (\zeta,\eta,\gamma) \to \infty$, *where* $\lambda_g \in \mathbb{C}$ *is independent of* $\zeta \in S^{p-1}$, $\eta \in S^{q-1}$.

ii) $(\psi g)(m) \to f_g$ *in *-strong operator topology when* $\gamma \to 0$, $m = (\zeta,\eta,\gamma)$, *where* $f_g \in C^*(V)$ *is independent of* $\zeta \in S^{p-1}$, $\eta \in S^{q-1}$. *Here* V *denotes the bilateral shift operator on* $L^2(\mathbb{R})$ *with respect to the orthonormal basis* $\{\ldots, f_{-1}, f_0, e_0, e_1, \ldots\}$ *defined in* (2.28), (2.29) *and* $C^*(V)$ *denotes the* C*-*algebra generated by* V. *and the identity.*

iii) *Recall that* $U = \hat{\mathbb{R}}^{p+q} - \{0\}$. *Let* σ *be the isomorphism of* C*-*algebras from* $C^*(V)$ *onto* $C_0(\mathbb{R})^+ \cong C(S^1)$ *determined by mapping* $V \mapsto 1+\theta$ *(see* (2.26)*). Then for the exact sequence* (2.4),

$$0 \to C^*(U,\mathcal{G}) \to C^*(G(p,q))^+ \xrightarrow{\pi_0} C_0(\mathbb{R})^+ \to 0$$

we have $\pi_0(g) = \sigma(f_g)$.

Proof. Obviously (i) follows from Corollary 3.2. We still use the notations defined in Theorem 2.5.

For the proof of (ii), it suffices to show that for any $g \in C^*(U,\mathcal{G})$ and for any polynomials in g_0, g_0^* that (ii) holds. We further notice that we may even assume $g \in C_c(\mathbb{R}, C_c(U))$, as $C_c(\mathbb{R}, C_c(U))$ is clearly a dense subalgebra of $C^*(U,\mathcal{G})$ and the remark at the beginning of the proof of Lemma 3.1 applies.

We may assume that $\tilde{g}(x,y,t) \equiv 0$ when $|(x,y,t)| > N$ or $|(x,y)| < \delta_0$ for some $N > 0$ and $\delta_0 > 0$. We show that for $m = (\zeta,\eta,\gamma)$,

$$\|\pi_m(g)\xi\| \to 0 \quad \text{as} \quad \gamma \to 0 \quad \text{for any} \quad \xi \in L^2(\mathbb{R}) .$$

Since $\|\pi_m(g)\|$ is uniformly bounded by $\|g\|$, we may as well assume that $\operatorname{supp}(\xi) \subseteq [-N,N]$ for N large. Then by (3.1),

$$\|\pi_m(g)\xi\|^2 = \int_{\mathbb{R}} \left| \int_{\mathbb{R}} (\tilde{g}(\gamma e^{-s}\zeta,\ \gamma e^{s}\eta,\ t)\xi(s-t)dt \right|^2 ds$$

(assumption on the last variable of $\tilde{g}$)
$$= \int_{\mathbb{R}} \left| \int_{-N}^{N} (\tilde{g}(\gamma e^{-s}\zeta,\ \gamma e^{s}\eta,\ t))\xi(s-t)dt \right|^2 ds$$

(assumption on ξ)
$$= \int_{-2N}^{2N} \left| \int_{-N}^{N} (\tilde{g}(\gamma e^{-s}\zeta,\ \gamma e^{s}\eta,\ t))\xi(s-t)dt \right|^2 ds = 0$$

when $\gamma < \delta_0 e^{-2N}$, by the assumption on the first p+q variables of $\tilde{g}$.

Recall that for $m = (\zeta,\eta,\gamma)$

$$(3.7) \qquad \pi_m(g_0)\xi(s) = -\hat{h}(\gamma e^{-}\ \zeta,\ \gamma e\ \eta) \int_0^{\infty} e^{-t/2}\xi(S-t)dt$$

where $\hat{h}$ satisfies that $\hat{h}(x,y) = 1$ when $|(x,y)| < 1$ and $\hat{h}(x,y) = 0$ when $|(x,y)| > \delta_1$, $\delta_1 > 1$.

Denote by V_0 the following operator on $L^2(\mathbb{R})$:

(3.8) $$V_0\xi(s) = -\int_0^\infty e^{-t/2}\,\xi(s-t)dt$$

We claim that

(3.9) $$\pi_m(g_0) \xrightarrow{*-st} V_0 \quad \text{as} \quad \gamma \to 0 .$$

For each $\gamma > 0$, define projections on $L^2(\mathbb{R})$ by multiplication operators:

(3.10) $$P_\gamma = M_{\chi_{[\ell n\,\gamma,\,\infty)}} ,$$

(3.11) $$Q = M_{\chi_{(-\infty,-\ell n\,\gamma]}} .$$

Then for every $\xi \in L^2(\mathbb{R})$ we have

(3.12) $$\| P_\gamma\xi - \xi \| \to 0 , \qquad \| Q_\gamma\xi - \xi \| \to 0 ,$$

$$\| P_\gamma Q_\gamma\xi - \xi \| = \| Q_\gamma P_\gamma\xi - \xi \| \to 0$$

when $\gamma \to 0^+$. By definition,

$$\hat{h}(\gamma e^{-s}\zeta,\ \gamma e^{s}\eta) = \begin{cases} 1 & |s| < -\ell n\ \gamma \\ 0 & |s| > \ell n\ \delta_1 - \ell n\ \gamma \end{cases}$$

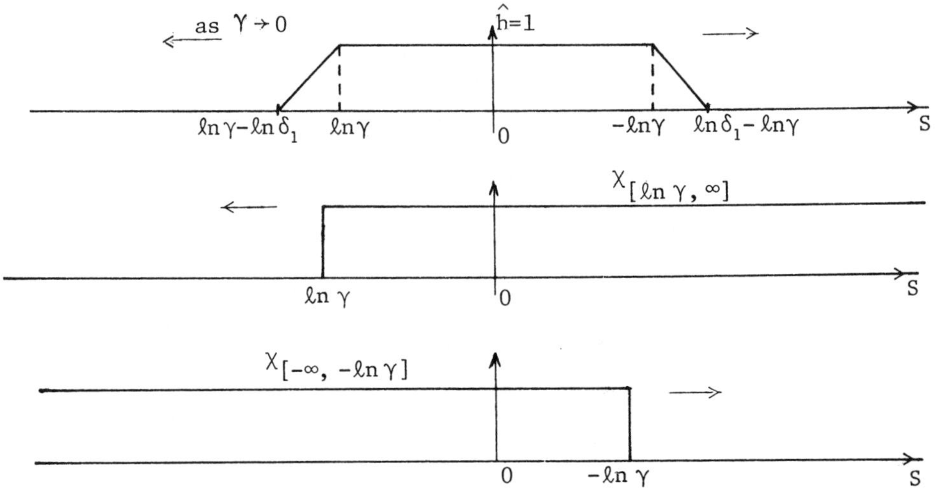

Figure 3.1

It is easy to see that

$$\| (M_{\hat{h}(\gamma e^{-\cdot}\zeta,\ \gamma e^{\cdot}\eta)} - P_\gamma Q_\gamma)\xi\| \to 0 \quad \text{as} \quad \gamma \to 0^+$$

for any $\xi \in L^2(\mathbb{R})$, and so

(3.13) $$M_{\hat{h}(\gamma e^{-\cdot}\zeta,\ \gamma e^{\cdot}\eta)} - P_\gamma Q_\gamma \xrightarrow{*-st} 0 \quad \text{as} \quad \gamma \to 0^+$$

As *-strong convergence is preserved under multiplication of a bounded operator,

(3.14) $$M_{\hat{h}(\gamma e^{-\cdot}\zeta,\ \gamma e^{\cdot}\eta)} V_0 - P_\gamma Q_\gamma V_0 \xrightarrow{*-st} 0 \quad \text{as} \quad \gamma \to 0^+ .$$

From (3.7) and (3.8),

(3.15) $$\pi_m(g_0) = M_{\hat{h}(\gamma e^{-\cdot}\zeta,\ \gamma e^{\cdot}\eta)} V_0 .$$

From (3.12)

(3.16) $$Q_\gamma P_\gamma V_0 - V_0 \xrightarrow{*-st} 0 .$$

Combine (3.14), (3.15) and (3.16) we obtain (3.9). So

(3.9') $$I + \pi_m(g_0) \xrightarrow{*-st} I + V_0 \quad \text{as} \quad \gamma \to 0^+ .$$

Since from (2.26)and (2.32)

$$I + V_0 = I + T + T' = (I + T) + (I + T') - I ,$$

one verifies from (2.31), (2.32), (2.34) and (2.36) that $I + V_0$ is nothing but exactly the bilateral shift operator V with respect to the orthonormal basis defined by (2.27) and (2.28).

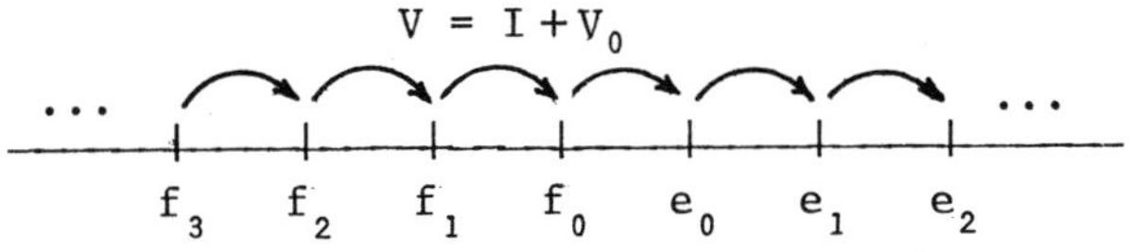

Figure 3.2

The net $\{\pi_m(g_0)\}$ is uniformly bounded so that (3.9) implies

$$\pi_m(g_0^2) \xrightarrow{*\text{-st}} V_0^2 \quad \text{as} \quad \gamma \to 0^+ \ .$$

By induction,

$$\pi_m(g_0^k) \xrightarrow{*\text{-st}} V_0^k \quad \text{as} \quad \gamma \to 0^+ \ .$$

Thus for any polynomial g in g_0 and g_0^*, (ii) holds. This finishes the proof of (ii).

Define a mapping π_0' by

$$C^*(G(p,q))^+ \longrightarrow C^*(V)$$

$$g \longmapsto f_g = *\text{-st} \lim_{\gamma \to 0} \pi_m(g) \ .$$

Then π_0' is obviously a homomorphism of C*-algebras.

The isomorphism σ from $C^*(V)$ onto $C_0(\mathbb{R})^+$ determined by sending V to $1+\theta$ makes the following diagram commute.

$$\begin{array}{ccc} & \overset{\pi_0'}{\nearrow} & C^*(V) \\ C^*(G(p,q))^+ & & \downarrow \sigma \\ & \underset{\pi_0}{\searrow} & C_0(\mathbb{R})^+ \cong C(S^1) \end{array} \ .$$

It follows that $\ker \pi_0' = \ker \pi_0 = C^*(U,\mathcal{Q})$ and

$$\pi_0(g) = \sigma \circ \pi_0'(g) = \sigma(f_g) \ . \qquad \text{Q.E.D.}$$

<u>Remark</u>. For $g \in C^*(G(p,q))$, $\pi_m(g)$ does not tend to 0 when $m \to 0$ in general. Consequently the natural embedding ψ in Theorem 3.3 does not represent $C^*(G(p,q))^+$ as a full algebra of operator fields over $S^{p-1} \times S^{q-1} \times (0,\infty)$. For the important notion of full algebras of operator fields, see J. M. G. Fell ([Fel]) And Y.Lee ([L1],[L2]). In §5 we will see that the limit $\lim\limits_{\gamma \to 0} \|\pi_{(\gamma\zeta,\gamma\eta)}(g)\|$ does exist for all $g \in C^*(G(p,q))$, although this limit almost never agrees with the norm of $\mathop{*\text{-st}\lim}\limits_{\gamma \to 0} \pi_{(\gamma\zeta,\gamma\eta)}(g)$ (which always exists by (ii) of Theorem 3.3). In fact, $\mathop{*\text{-st}\lim}\limits_{\gamma \to 0} \pi_{(\gamma\zeta,\gamma\eta)}(g)$ is always 0 for $g \in C^*(U,\mathcal{G})$ but one cannot hope that $\pi_{(\gamma\zeta,\gamma\eta)}(g) \to 0$ in norm when $\gamma \to 0$ for all $g \in C^*(U,\mathcal{G})$. We don't want to elaborate on this but it will become transparent after the structure theorems have been proved in §5.

Theorem 3.3 showed explicitly how the C*-algebra $C(S^1) \simeq C^*(U)$ is "attached" to one corner of the boundary of $S^{p-1} \times S^{q-1} \times (0,\infty)$ when we consider $C^*(G(p,q))^+$ as a subalgebra of $C^b(S^{p-1} \times S^{q-1} \times (0,\infty),\mathcal{K})$. This helped us to understand the extension (2.5), although up to this point the structure of the ideal $C^*(U,\mathcal{G})$ is still a mystery. Understanding that will be our task in the next section.

§4. THE IDEALS: C*-ALGEBRAS OF FOLIATIONS

Recall from (2.4), (2.5) and (2.6) that there is an exact sequence

(4.1) $$0 \to C_0(S^{p-1} \times S^{q-1} \times (0,\infty), \mathcal{K}) \to C^*(U,\mathcal{G}) \xrightarrow{\pi_x} C(S^{p-1} \cup S^{q-1}, \mathcal{K}) \to 0 .$$

In this section we shall identify the element represented by the extension (4.1) in the group $KK^1(C(S^{p-1} \cup S^{q-1}, \mathcal{K}), C\ (S^{p-1} \times S^{q-1} \times (0,\infty), \mathcal{K})$ and determine explicitly the structure of the C*-algebra $C^*(U,\mathcal{G})$ of foliation. It turns out that the C*-algebra $C^*(U,\mathcal{G})$ admits a nice simple description which will provide us with much of the preparation for studying the structure of $C^*(G(p,q))$ in the next section.

While computing the elements of KK^1-groups, in order to exhibit a geometric aspect of the problem, we call the reader's attention to its connection to a similar situation in Reeb foliation ([Tor], Thm. 3.4.1) and give a rather detailed discussion in this connection for the special case p=q=1, which yields Theorem 4.1 and Corollary 4.2. However the method used in the study of the structure of $C^*(U,\mathcal{G})$ in the second part of this section is entirely different and is very useful in other situations (see Theorem 4.1.2, Part II of this thesis). In fact the element represented by the extension (4.1) in the KK^1-group will be easily determined from the structure of $C^*(U,\mathcal{G})$ and thus obtain in particular an alternative proof of Theorem 4.1 and Corollary 4.2.

Fix $P \in S^{p-1}$, $Q \in S^{q-1}$ and consider a C*-algebra of the foliation $\mathcal{G}$ in the quarter plane S_{PQ} with the boundary except the origin. See Figure 4.1. The foliation is given by the hyperbolic flows. By "pulling" the origin to $-\infty$, it is easy to see that this foliated manifold

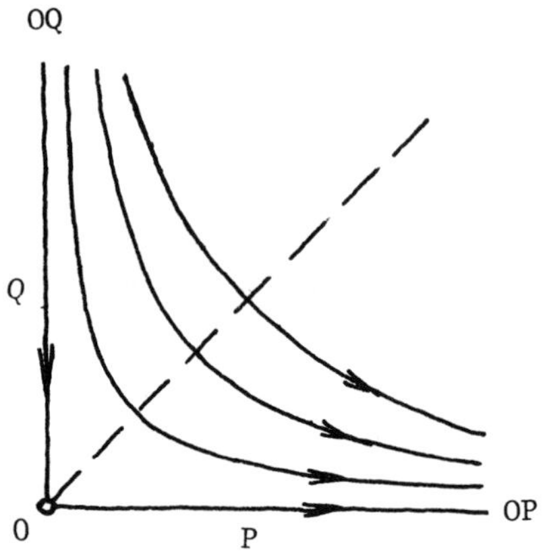

Figure 4.1

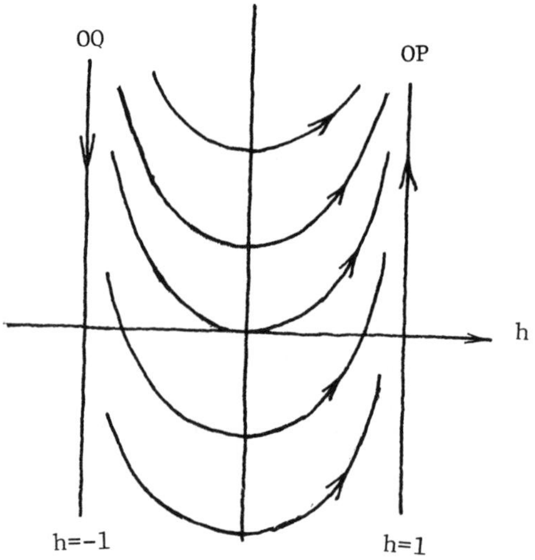

Figure 4.2

is diffeomorphic to the infinite strip $[-1,1]\times\mathbb{R}$ in the (h,y) plane foliated by the lines $h=\pm 1$ and graphs of the functions $y = f(h)+c$ $-1<h<1$, $\lim_{x\to\pm 1} f(h) = \infty$, as shown in Figure 4.2. By Proposition 1.4 we have

$$(4.2) \qquad 0 \to C^*(\mathring{S}_{PQ},\mathcal{F}) \to C^*(S_{PQ},\mathcal{F}) \xrightarrow{\pi_{PQ}} C^*(\mathcal{L},\mathcal{F}) \longrightarrow 0$$

where $\mathring{S}_{PQ}$ is the interior and $\mathcal{L} = OP \cup OQ$ is the boundary. Taking the y-axis as a transversal for $(\mathring{S}_{PQ},\mathcal{F})$ we see that $C^*(\mathring{S}_{PQ},\mathcal{F}) \cong C_0(\mathbb{R}) \otimes K(L^2(\mathbb{R}))$. It is also clear that $C^*(\mathcal{L},\mathcal{F}) \cong \mathcal{K}(L^2(\mathbb{R}))^2$, hence

$$(4.2') \qquad 0 \longrightarrow C_0(\mathbb{R})\otimes\mathcal{K} \longrightarrow C^*(S_{PQ},\mathcal{F}) \xrightarrow{\pi_{PQ}} \mathcal{K}^2 \longrightarrow 0 \quad .$$

This extension determines an element of $KK^1(K^2, C_0(\mathbb{R})\otimes\mathcal{K}) \cong KK^1(\mathbb{C}^2, C_0(\mathbb{R})) \cong KK^0(\mathbb{C}^2,\mathbb{C}) \cong \mathbb{Z}^2$.

Let's consider the associated six-term exact sequence of (4.2'):

$$(4.3) \qquad \begin{array}{ccccc}
0 \cong K_0(C_0(\mathbb{R})\otimes\mathcal{K}) & \longrightarrow & K_0(C^*(S_{PQ},\mathcal{F})) \cong \mathbb{Z} & \longrightarrow & K_0(\mathcal{K}^2) \cong \mathbb{Z}^2 \\
\uparrow & & & & \downarrow \\
0 \cong K_1(\mathcal{K}^2) & \longleftarrow & K_1(C^*(S_{PQ},\mathcal{F})) \cong 0 & \longleftarrow & K_1(C_0(\mathbb{R})\otimes\mathcal{K}) \cong \mathbb{Z}
\end{array}$$

where

$$K_0(C^*(S_{PQ},\mathcal{F})) \simeq K^1([-1,1]\times\mathbb{R}) \simeq \mathbb{Z}$$
$$K_1(C^*(S_{PQ},\mathcal{F})) \simeq K^0([-1,1]\times\mathbb{R}) \simeq 0 \quad .$$

by Connes' analogue of the Thom isomorphism ([Con]).

The element of the KK^1-group is determined by the exponential map

$$\text{(4.4)} \qquad KK^1(\mathcal{K}^2, C_0(\mathbb{R})\otimes\mathcal{K}) \simeq \mathrm{Hom}(K_0(\mathcal{K}^2), K_1(C_0(\mathbb{R})\otimes\mathcal{K}) \quad .$$

Now let's specify the generators for the above K-groups. Let $p \in C_c^\infty(\mathbb{R})$ be a "bump" function with support in $(-\varepsilon,\varepsilon)$, $\int_{\mathbb{R}} |p(t)|^2\,dt = 1$. The integral operator on $L^2(\mathbb{R})$ with kernel function $p(x)\overline{p(y)}$ is a rank-1 projection in $\mathcal{K}(L^2(\mathbb{R}))$. Under the isomorphism $\mathcal{K}(L^2(\mathbb{R})) \cong C_0(\mathbb{R}) \rtimes \mathbb{R}$, it corresponds to $P \in C_c(\mathbb{R}^2) \subset C_0(\mathbb{R}) \rtimes \mathbb{R}$ where

$$P(s,t) = p(s)\overline{p(s-t)} \quad .$$

The isomorphism $K_0(C_0(\mathbb{R}) \rtimes \mathbb{R}) \simeq \mathbb{Z}$ is given by the natural trace

$$\mathrm{Tr}(f) = \int_{\mathbb{R}} f(s,0)\,ds \quad , \qquad f \in C_c(\mathbb{R}^2) \subset C_0(\mathbb{R}) \rtimes \mathbb{R} \quad .$$

Here $K_0(C^*(\mathcal{L},\mathcal{G})) \simeq K_0((C_0(\mathbb{R}) \rtimes \mathbb{R})^2) \simeq \mathbb{Z}^2$ has two generators corresponding to two copies of $\mathbb{R}$, OP and OQ. Each generator is given by the class of the above P.

There is also a canonical generator for the following K_1-group:

$$K_1(C_0(0,\infty) \otimes \mathcal{K}(L^2(\mathbb{R}))) \simeq K_1(C_0(0,\infty)^+ \otimes \mathcal{K}(L^2(\mathbb{R}))) \simeq \mathbb{Z}$$

namely, the class of $v \otimes P + 1 \otimes (I-P)$ where $v \in C_0(0,\infty)^+$ has the form $v(t) = e^{2\pi i\phi(t)}$ for $\phi \in C^b(0,\infty)$ with

$$\lim_{t\to 0} \phi(t) = 0 \quad , \qquad \lim_{t\to\infty} \phi(t) = 1 \quad .$$

The isomorphism $K_1(C_0(0,\infty)^+ \otimes \mathcal{K}(L^2(\mathbb{R}))) \simeq \mathbb{Z}$, with respect to the generator $[v \otimes P + 1 \otimes (I-P)]$ is given by the winding number. If $[V] \in K_1(C_0(0,\infty)^+ \otimes \mathcal{K})$ is represented by a differentiable loop $V\colon (0,\infty)^+ \longrightarrow \{\text{trace class operators}\} \subset \mathcal{K}$ then the winding number of [V] is

$$W_V = \frac{1}{2\pi_i} \int^{\infty} Tr(V'(t) \circ V(t)^{-1})dt$$

where $(0,\infty)^+$ is the one-point compactification of $(0,\infty)$. The reader is referred to [Torpe, Lemma 3.3.4] for the above formulas.

THEOREM 4.1. *Given the basis for the* K*-groups as above, the exponential map in* (4.3) *is given by* $(n,m) \mapsto -n-m$ *for* $(n,m) \in \mathbb{Z}^2 \simeq K_0(\mathcal{K}^2)$. *Therefore the element represented by the extension* (4.2) *is* $(-1,-1)$ *in* $KK^1(K^2, C_0(\mathbb{R}) \otimes \mathcal{K})$ *(see* (4.4)*). In particular, the short exact sequence* (4.2) *is not stably split.*

Proof. We use the foliated infinite strip $[-1,1] \times \mathbb{R}$ as the model for $(S_{PQ}, \mathcal{F})$. See Figure 4.2. In the interior $\mathring{S}_{PQ}$ the foliation is given by a family of curves $y = \alpha(h) + C$, $h \in (-1,1)$, $-\infty < C < \infty$. For convenience, we may assume that

$$\alpha(h) = \sec(\pi h/2) \quad .$$

For any saturated submanifold M of S_{PQ}, we denote $G(M)$ the graph of the foliation $(M, \mathcal{F})$.

Consider the exact sequence (4.2). Let $f \in C_c(G(\mathcal{L})) \subset C^*(\mathcal{L}, \mathcal{F})$. We want to find a preimage $F_f \in \pi_{PQ}^{-1}(f)$ in $C_c(G(S_{PQ})) \subset C^*(S_{PQ}, \mathcal{F})$. Assume at first that $supp(f) \subset G(OP)$. Identify $G(OP)$ with $\mathbb{R}^2$ by the mapping $\gamma \mapsto (S(\gamma), r(\gamma))$. Then $f \in C_c(\mathbb{R}^2)$ and there is some $N > 0$ such that $supp(f) \subset B_N$, the disk of radius N centered at $0 \in \mathbb{R}^2$.

Let

$$S_{PQ}^{+} = \{(h,y) \in S_{PQ} \mid h > 0\}$$
$$S_{PQ}^{-} = \{(h,y) \in S_{PQ} \mid h < 0\}$$

be two open submanifolds of S_{PQ}. Let $G(S^+_{PQ}) = \{\gamma \in G(S_{PQ}) \mid \gamma \subset S^+_{PQ}\}$. Then $G(S^+_{PQ})$ is also the graph of the restriction of the foliation to S^+_{PQ}. For $\gamma \in G(S^+_{PQ})$, let the source $S(\gamma) = (h_0, y_0)$ and the range $r(\gamma) = (h_1, y_1)$, (see Figure 4.3), be the mapping $\gamma \mapsto (h_0, y_0, y_1)$ identifying $G(S^+_{PQ})$ with an open subset of $(0,1] \times \mathbb{R} \times \mathbb{R}$.

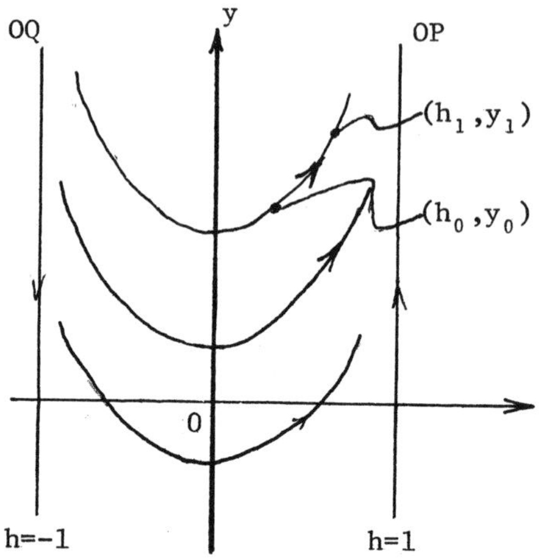

Figure 4.3

For the given $F \in C_c(G(OP))$, we want to find a preimage $F_f \in C_c(G(S_{PQ}))$ along with a flow coordinate system for $G(S_{PQ})$ such that F_f has extremely simple form with respect to this system so its exponential can be easily computed. We are going to "adapt" locally a patch of Euclidean coordinates into flow coordinates. Fix $\varepsilon_0 \in (0,1)$. We choose a transversal for $\mathring{S}_{PQ} \subset OP$ by an interval RT (which coincides with $[\varepsilon_0, 1]$ on h-axis), a quarter circle of radius $-\varepsilon_0/2$ and a ray parallel to y-axis; see Figure 4.5. The transversal coordinate s of a leaf L is the geodesic length from the intersection to R. The leaf with coordinate S is denoted by L_S. Of course OP corresponds to S=0.

Let σ_t, $t \in \mathbb{R}$ be a 1-parameter transformation group on S_{PQ} which determines the flows. We may assume that the vector field is invariant under vertical translation and that the y-component of the vector field on the thin strip $\varepsilon_0 \leq h \leq 1$ $(-1 \leq h \leq -\varepsilon_0)$ is constant 1

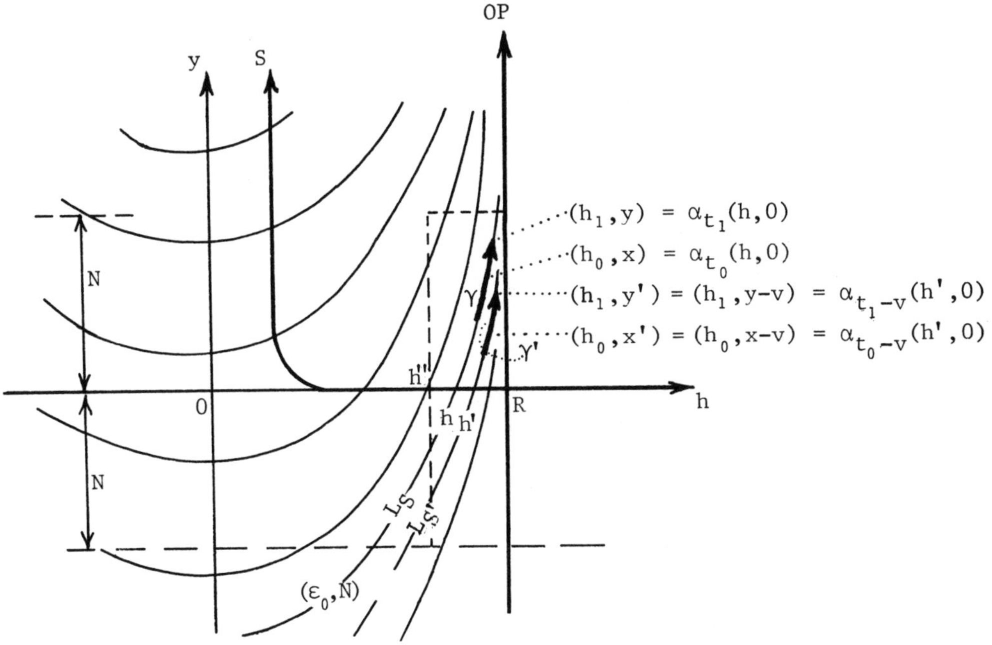

Figure 4.4

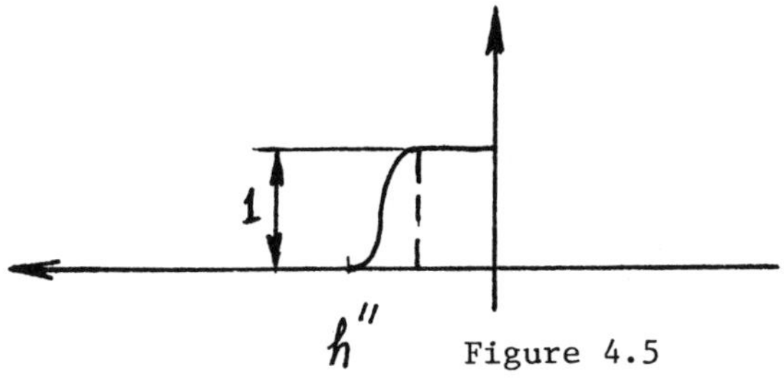

Figure 4.5

(-1, resp.). Therefore for any $\varepsilon_0 \le h_0 \le 1$, we have

$$\sigma_t(h_0,y) = (h_1, y+t) \quad , \qquad t \in \mathbb{R} \tag{4.5}$$

whenever h_0,h_1 are inside $[\varepsilon_0,1]$.

Let h" be the transversal coordinate of the leaf containing (ε_0,N), where we recall that $\text{supp}(f) \subset B_N$. Pick a leaf L_S, $h'' < S < 1$. Let γ be any path contained in L_S. There are $t_0,t_1 \in \mathbb{R}$ such that

$$\sigma_{t_0}(h,0) = s(\gamma) \quad , \qquad \sigma_{t_1}(h,0) = r(\gamma) \tag{4.6}$$

where (h,0) is the intersection of L_S with the positive h-axis, h=S. We define a flow coordinate by

$$\Phi(\gamma) = (S,t_0,t_1) \quad . \tag{4.7}$$

Let

$$s(\gamma) = (h_0,x) \quad , \qquad r(\gamma) = (h_1,y) \quad . \tag{4.8}$$

Suppose that h_0,h_1 are the interval $[\varepsilon_0,1]$, then by (4.5) we have

$$x = t_0 \quad , \qquad y = t_1 \quad . \tag{4.9}$$

Now let $\gamma' \subset L_{S'}$ be another path with

$$s(\gamma') = (h_0,x') \quad , \qquad r(\gamma') = (h_1,y') \tag{4.10}$$

then a vertical translation by v brings γ' to γ (see (4.8)) where

$$v = x - x' = y - y' \quad . \tag{4.11}$$

We define (compare (4.7))

$$\Phi(\gamma') = (S', t_0-v, t_1-v) \quad . \tag{4.12}$$

Let the intersection of $L_{S'}$ with the positive h-axis be $(h',0)$ (if such an intersection exists). It is clear that if $h_0, h_1, h' \in [\varepsilon_0, 1]$ then

$$\alpha_{t_0-v}(h',0) = (h_0, x') = s(\gamma')$$
$$\alpha_{t_1-v}(h',0) = (h_1, y') = r(\gamma') \quad .$$

By (4.12) we see that the flow coordinates Φ are independent on the first L_S we pick.

Define a C^∞-function ρ such that

$$(4.13) \qquad \rho(S) = \begin{cases} 1 & S \le h''/2 \\ 0 & S \ge h'' \end{cases}$$

as shown in Figure 4.5.

Now the function F_f on $G(S_{PQ})$ can be defined by

$$(4.14) \qquad F_f(\gamma) = \begin{cases} 0 & \text{if } \gamma \in G(S^+_{PQ}) \\ \rho(S) f(x,y) & \text{if } \gamma \in G(S^+_{PQ}),\ \gamma \subset L_S \\ & \quad s(\gamma) = (h_0, x),\ r(\gamma) = (h_1, y) \ . \end{cases}$$

It is clear that $F_f \in C^\infty_c(G(S_{PQ}))$.

If $F_f(\gamma) \neq 0$ for certain $\gamma \subset L_S$, $s(\gamma) = (h_0, x)$, $r(\gamma) = (h_1, y)$ then $0 \le S \le h''$ by (4.13), $(x,y) \in \mathrm{supp}(f) \subset D_N$ also. Because of the way we choose h'', we have $h_0, h_1 \in [\varepsilon_0, 1]$. From (4.9), $t_0 = x$, $t_1 = y$ hold. So the same F_f can be defined by

$$(4.15) \qquad F_f(\gamma) = \begin{cases} 0 & \text{if } \gamma \in G(S^+_{PQ}) \\ \rho(S) f(t_0, t_1) & \text{if } \gamma \in G(S^+_{PQ}),\ \Phi(\gamma) = (S, t_0, t_1). \end{cases}$$

In particular, if $f = P$ is a rank-1 projection in

$C^*(OP) \cong \mathcal{K}(L^2(\mathbb{R}))$, $P(x,y) = p(x)\bar{p}(x-y)$, where $p \in C_c(\mathbb{R})$, $\int_{\mathbb{R}} |p(x)|^2 dx$, $\operatorname{supp}(P) \subseteq D_N$, then we have a preimage $F_P \in \pi_{PQ}^{-1}(P)$

$$(4.16) \qquad F_P(\gamma) = \begin{cases} 0 & \text{if } \gamma \in G(S_{PQ}^+) \\ \rho(s)p(h)\bar{p}(t_0-t_1) & \text{if } \gamma \in S_{PQ}^+, \quad \Phi(\gamma) = (s,t_0,t_1) . \end{cases}$$

Let π_s be the irreducible representation of $C^*(S_{PQ},\mathcal{G})$ on $L^2(G_{P_s}) \cong L^2(\mathbb{R})$ where $P_s \in S_{PQ}$ is the intersection of the transversal and L_s. Refer to §1 for notation. Then (1.5) shows

$$\pi_s(F_P) = \rho(s)P \quad , \qquad 0 \leq s < \infty \quad .$$

Therefore

$$\begin{aligned} \pi_s(\exp(2\pi i F_P)) &= \exp(2\pi i \pi_s(F_P)) \\ &= \exp(2\pi i \rho(s))P + (1-P) \quad . \end{aligned}$$

The winding number of $\exp(2\pi i\rho)$ is

$$W = \frac{1}{2\pi i} \int_0^\infty \frac{(\exp 2\pi i\rho(s))'}{\exp 2\pi i\rho(s)} ds = -1 \quad .$$

Hence

$$\delta_0[P] = [\exp 2\pi i F_P] = -1$$

in $K_1(C^*(S_{PQ},\mathcal{G})) \cong K_1(C_0(0,\infty) \otimes \mathcal{K}(L^2(\mathbb{R})))$ with respect to the basis we specified before.

Analogously for $P \in C_c(G(OQ))$. Q.E.D.

<u>Remark.</u> We have a K-theoretic six-term exact sequence associated to (4.1):

$$
(4.17)\qquad
\begin{array}{ccccc}
K^0(S^{p-1}\times S^{q-1}\times(0,\infty)) & \longrightarrow & K^0(C^*(U,\mathcal{G})) & \longrightarrow & K^0(S^{p-1}\cup S^{q-1}) \\
\uparrow{\scriptstyle\delta_1} & & & & \downarrow{\scriptstyle\delta_0} \\
K^2(S^{p-1}\times S^{q-1}) & \longleftarrow & K^1(C^*(U,\mathcal{G})) & \longleftarrow & K^1(S^{p-1}\times S^{q-1}\times(0,\infty))
\end{array}
$$

Since the K-groups involved are torsion-free, again by the universal coefficient theorem ([R-S]), the element in $KK^1(C(S^{p-1}\cup S^{q-1},\mathcal{K}),$ $C_0(S^{p-1}\times S^{q-1}\times(0,\infty), M_2(\mathcal{K}))$ represented by the extension (4.1) is given by the exponential map δ_0 and the index map δ_1.

When p=q=1, we fix a basis $\{e_{p,1}, e_{p,2}, e_{q,1}, e_{q,2}\}$ for $K^0(C(S^0\cup S^0,\mathcal{K}))$ as in the paragraph preceding Proposition 2.4. Then a basis of $K^1(C_0(S^0\times S^0\times(0,\infty), M_2(\mathcal{K}))$ can be written as $\{[e_{p,1}]\boxtimes[e_{q,1}]\boxtimes(-b), [e_{p,1}]\boxtimes[e_{q,2}]\boxtimes(-b), [e_{p,2}]\boxtimes[e_{q,1}]\boxtimes(-b),$ $[e_{p,2}]\boxtimes[e_{q,2}]\boxtimes(-b)\}$, where $\boxtimes$ stands for the external product of K-groups and b is the canonical generator of $K_1(C_0(0,1))$ ([C1], p.51). With these bases (4.17) becomes

$$
\begin{array}{ccccc}
0 & \longrightarrow & \mathbb{Z} & \longrightarrow & \mathbb{Z}^4 \\
{\scriptstyle 0=\delta_1}\uparrow & & & & \downarrow{\scriptstyle\delta_0} \\
0 & \longleftarrow & \mathbb{Z} & \longleftarrow & \mathbb{Z}^4
\end{array}\quad .
$$

An easy corollary of Theorem 4.1 is

COROLLARY 4.2. *With* p=q=1, *with the bases given as above the element* $\delta_0 \in \mathrm{Hom}(K^0(S^0\cup S^0), K^1(S^0\times S^0\times(0,1)) \simeq KK^1(C(S^0\cup S^0,\mathcal{K}),$ $C_0(S^0\times S^0\times(0,1), M_2(\mathcal{K}))$ *represented by the exact sequence* (4.1) *is*

$$\delta_0 = \begin{pmatrix} -1 & -1 & 0 & 0 \\ 0 & 0 & -1 & -1 \\ -1 & 0 & -1 & 0 \\ 0 & -1 & 0 & -1 \end{pmatrix}$$

Now we consider the general situation.

THEOREM 4.3. *The* C^**-algebra of foliation* $C^*(U,\mathcal{G})$ *is isomorphic to the* C^**-algebra*

$$A_U = \left\{ f \in C_0(S^{p-1} \times S^{q-1} \times [0,1), M_2(\mathcal{K})) \mid f(x,y,0) = \begin{pmatrix} f_1(x) & 0 \\ 0 & f_2(y) \end{pmatrix}, \; f_1(x),\ f_2(y) \in \mathcal{K} \right\}. \tag{4.18}$$

Furthermore the isomorphism ψ_U *is canonical in the sense that the following diagram commutes (see* (2.7), (2.8) *and* (4.1)*):*

$$\begin{array}{ccccccccc} 0 & \longrightarrow & C_1^*(U_1,\mathcal{G}) & \longrightarrow & C^*(U,\mathcal{G}) & \longrightarrow & C^*(X,\mathcal{G}) & \longrightarrow & 0 \\ & & \downarrow \psi_{U_1} \simeq & & \downarrow \psi_U \simeq & & \downarrow \psi_X \simeq & & \\ 0 & \rightarrow & C_0(S^{p-1}\times S^{q-1}\times(0,1),\mathcal{K}) & \xrightarrow{i_{U_1}} & A_U & \xrightarrow{\pi'_X} & C(S^{p-1}\cup S^{q-1},\mathcal{K}) & \longrightarrow & 0 \end{array} \tag{4.19}$$

where i_U *is the inclusion and* π'_X *is the restriction sending* f *to* $f_1 \cup f_2$ *(see* (4.18)*)*

<u>Proof</u>. The idea of the proof is analogous to that of Theorem 4.1.2 in [W1]. For the details omitted from the following discussion the reader is referred there.

Let $H_U = S^{p-1} \times S^{q-1} \times [0,1) \times \mathbb{R}$. The canonical submersion of H_U onto $S^{p-1} \times S^{q-1} \times [0,1)$ induces a foliation $(H_U,\mathcal{G})$. Its graph $G(H_U,\mathcal{G}) \simeq S^{p-1} \times S^{q-1} \times [0,1) \times \mathbb{R}^2$ with the composition law

$$(\alpha,x,y)(\alpha,y,z) = (\alpha,x,z) \tag{4.20}$$

for $\alpha \in S^{p-1} \times S^{q-1} \times [0,1)$. Let $f \in C_c(G(H_U,\mathcal{F})) \subset C^*(H_U,\mathcal{F})$. The formula

$$(4.21) \qquad \psi f_\alpha \xi(x) = \int_{\mathbb{R}} f(\alpha,x,y)\xi(y)\,dy$$

defines an operator ψf_α on $L^2(\mathbb{R})$. The mapping $f \mapsto (\alpha \mapsto \psi f_\alpha)$ extends to a canonical isomorphism ψ between $C^*(H_U,\mathcal{F})$ and $C_0(S^{p-1} \times S^{q-1} \times [0,1), \mathcal{K}(L^2(\mathbb{R})))$ (Proposition 1.3). Corresponding to $L^2(\mathbb{R}) \simeq L^2(\mathbb{R}^+) \oplus L^2(\mathbb{R}^-)$, we have $\mathcal{K}(L^2(\mathbb{R})) = M_2(\mathcal{K})$ and

$$C^*(H_U,\mathcal{F}) \simeq C_0(S^{p-1} \times S^{q-1} \times [0,1), M_2(\mathcal{K})) \quad .$$

With the same composition law (4.20), the graph of the foliation is

$$(4.22) \qquad \mathbb{G}(U,\mathcal{F}) = \left\{(\zeta,\eta,t,x,y) \in S^{p-1} \times S^{q-1} \times [0,1) \times \mathbb{R}^2 \;\middle|\; \begin{matrix}\text{if } t=0 \\ \text{then } x\cdot y > 0\end{matrix}\right\}$$

which is an open subgroupoid of $\mathbb{G}(H_U,\mathcal{F})$. The inclusion $C_c(\mathbb{G}(U,\mathcal{F})) \subset C_c(\mathbb{G}(H_U,\mathcal{F}))$ extends to an imbedding τ from $C^*(U,\mathcal{F})$ into $C^*(H_U,\mathcal{F})$. Let $f \in C_c(\mathbb{G}(U,\mathcal{F}))$. Then $\tau f \in C_c(\mathbb{G}(H_U,\mathcal{F}))$ satisfies $\tau f(\zeta,\eta,0,x,y) = 0$ if $xy \leq 0$; see (4.22). From the formula (4.21) we can easily check that both $L^2(\mathbb{R}^+)$ and $L^2(\mathbb{R}^-)$ are invariant under the action of $\psi(\tau f_{(\zeta,\eta,0)})$. Thus $\psi\cdot\tau(C^*(U,\mathcal{F})) \subset A_U$. Now we apply a C*-algebraic version of the Stone-Weierstrass theorem to verify that $\psi_U = \psi\cdot\tau$ is an isomorphism of $C^*(U,\mathcal{F})$ onto A_U. The commutativity of the diagram (4.19) follows from the definition of the isomorphism ψ_U and a diagram chasing. Q.E.D.

It is now quite easy to compute the KK^1-element represented by (4.1). First we recall some familiar notation. Let A be any unital

C*-algebra. By definition the suspension SA of A and the cone CA over A are

$$SA = C_0((0,1),\ A) \quad , \qquad CA = C_0([0,1),\ A) \quad .$$

Their unitalizations

$$\begin{aligned} (SA)^+ &= \{f \in C([0,1],\ A) \mid f(0) = f(1) \in \mathbb{C}\cdot 1_A\} \\ (CA)^+ &= \{f \in C([0,1],\ A) \mid f(1) \in \mathbb{C}\cdot 1_A\} \end{aligned}$$

See ([C1], VI.1). Associated to the exact sequence

$$(4.23) \qquad 0 \longrightarrow SA \longrightarrow CA \longrightarrow A \longrightarrow 0$$

there are connecting maps $S_A^0\colon K_0(A) \to K_1(SA)$ and $S_A^1\colon K_1(A) \longrightarrow K_0(SA)$ called the suspension isomorphisms which have explicit forms ([C1], Lemma 1, pg.50). Let j be the obvious inclusion $C(S^{p-1} \cup S^{q-1}, \mathcal{K}) \hookrightarrow C(S^{p-1} \times S^{q-1}, M_2(\mathcal{K}))$ and j_*^i, i=0,1, the induced K-group homomorphisms.

COROLLARY 4.4. *The connecting homomorphisms* δ_i, i=0,1, *in* (4.17) *are given by* $\delta_i = S^i \circ j_*^i$, i=1,2. *Here* $S^i = S_A^i$ *are the suspension isomorphisms for* $A_x = C(S^{p-1} \times S^{q-1}, M_2(\mathcal{K}))$.

Proof. From (4.19) we have the following commuting diagram (write $A = A_x$):

$$\begin{array}{ccccccccc} 0 \to & C_0(S^{p-1}\times S^{q-1}\times (0,1), M_2(\mathcal{K})) & \to & C^*(U,\mathcal{G}) & \to & C(S^{p-1}\cup S^{q-1},\mathcal{K}) & \to 0 \\ & \| & & \simeq\downarrow j_U\circ\psi_U & & \downarrow j & \\ 0 \longrightarrow & SA & \longrightarrow & CA & \xrightarrow{\ \sigma\ } & A & \longrightarrow 0 \end{array}$$

(4.24)

where j_{U_1} is the inclusion of A_U onto CA and we have identified ψ_{U_1} and ψ_x with their images.

Since the connecting homomorphisms are natural, the following diagram commutes:

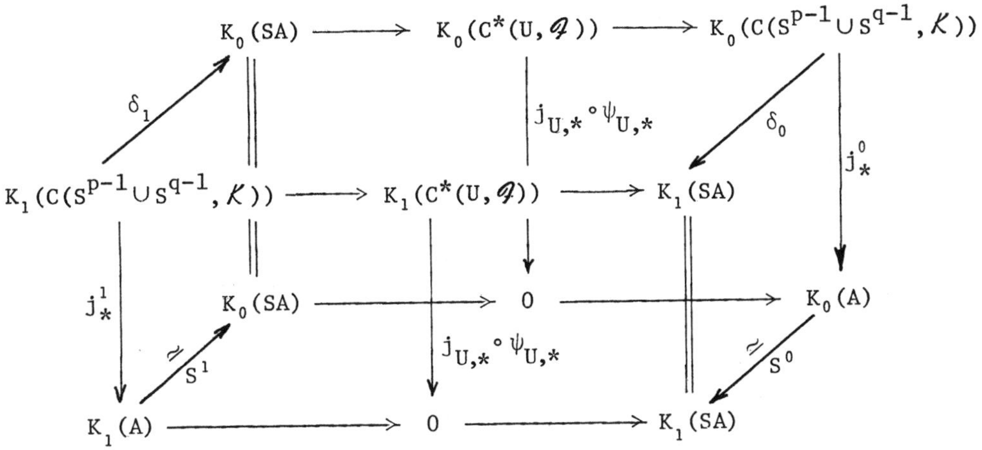

The corollary follows from this. Q.E.D.

COROLLARY 4.5. *Retain the notation in Corollary 4.4.*

(i) *Let* f *be a continuous function from* $[0,1]$ *to* $\mathbb{C}^*$ *with* $f(0) = f(1) = 1$, *and winding number* 1, *let* $e \in \text{Proj } M_n(C(S^{p-1} \cup S^{q-1}, \mathcal{K})) \subset \text{Proj } M_n(A)$. *Then* $\delta_0([e]) \in K_1(SA)$ *is the class of* $1 + (f-1) \otimes e \in GL_n((SA)^+)$.

(ii) *Let* $t \to R(t)$ *be a continuous map of* $[0,1]$ *to* $U(2) \subset M_2(\mathbb{C})$ *with* $R(a) = \begin{pmatrix} 1 & 0 \\ 0 & 1 \end{pmatrix}$, $R(b) = \begin{pmatrix} 0 & -1 \\ 1 & 0 \end{pmatrix}$. *For any* $u \in U_n(C(S^{p-1} \cup S^{q-1}, \mathcal{K})) \subset U_n(A)$ *we have* $\delta_1([u]) = [e] - [e_0]$ *where* $e_0, e \in \text{Proj } M_{2n}(A)$ *are the following*

$$e_0(t) = \begin{pmatrix} 1 & 0 \\ 0 & 1 \end{pmatrix}, \quad t \in [0,1], \quad e(t) = W(t)e_0(t)W(t)^*,$$

$$W(t) = R(t)\begin{pmatrix} U^{-1} & 0 \\ 0 & 1 \end{pmatrix} R(t)^* .$$

Proof. It follows from Theorem 4.4 above and Lemma 1 of [C1].

Q.E.D.

Example 4.6. Now we can show how Corollary 4.2 follows easily from Theorems 4.3 and 4.4. Let p=q=1 as in Theorem 4.4. Let us compute the exponential map δ_0, which is in $\mathrm{Hom}(\mathbb{Z}^4, \mathbb{Z}^4)$ in terms of the bases of the K-groups fixed as in Corollary 4.2. We put $S_p^0 = \{x_1, x_2\}$, $S_q^0 = \{y_1, y_2\}$ for the two S^0. The projection $e_{p,1} \in C(S_p^0 \cup S_q^0, \mathcal{K})$, $e_{p,1} = \chi_{x_1} \cdot p_0$ (p_0 is a rank-1 projection in $\mathcal{K}$), is mapped by the inclusion j to the following projection:

$$je_{p,1}(x_1, y_i) = p_0 , \qquad je_{p,1}(x_2, y_i) = 0$$

for i=1,2. Thus

$$je_{p,1} = \begin{pmatrix} e_{p,1}\chi_{y_1} & 0 \\ 0 & 0 \end{pmatrix} + \begin{pmatrix} e_{p,1}\chi_{y_2} & 0 \\ 0 & 0 \end{pmatrix}$$

and by Theorem 4.4 above and Corollary 3 of [C1],

$$\begin{aligned} \delta_0([e_{p,1}]) &= S^0 \cdot j_*([e_{p,1}]) \\ &= S^0([e_{p,1}] \boxtimes [e_{q,1}] \oplus [e_{p,1}] \boxtimes [e_{q,2}]) \\ &= [e_{p,1}] \boxtimes [e_{q,1}] \boxtimes b \oplus [e_{p,1}] \boxtimes [e_{q,2}] \boxtimes b . \end{aligned}$$

Similarly for $[e_{p,2}]$, $[e_{q,1}]$ and $[e_{q,2}]$. Now Corollary 4.2 follows.

Example 4.7. Now we let p=2, q=1. In this case both the index map and the exponential map are nonzero. The six-term exact sequence is

$$\begin{array}{ccccc}
K^0(S^1 \times S^0 \times (0,1)) & \longrightarrow & K_0(C^*(U,\mathcal{G})) & \longrightarrow & K^0(S^1 \cup S^0) \\
\uparrow \delta_1 & & & & \downarrow \delta_0 \\
K^1(S^1 \cup S^0) & \longrightarrow & K_1(C^*(U,\mathcal{G})) & \longrightarrow & K^1(S^1 \times S^0 \times (0,1))
\end{array} .$$

By Connes' analogue of the Thom isomorphism we easily compute $K_0(C^*(U,\mathcal{G})) \simeq \mathbb{Z}^2$, $K_1(C^*(U,\mathcal{G})) \simeq 0$. As usual we fix bases of the K-groups as follows:

$$K_0(C(S^1 \cup S^0, \mathcal{K})) \simeq \mathbb{Z}^3 \qquad \{[e_p], [e_{q,1}], [e_{q,2}]\}$$

$$K_1(C_0(S^1 \times S^0 \times (0,\infty), \mathcal{K})) \simeq \mathbb{Z}^2 , \{[e_p] \boxtimes [e_{q,1}] \boxtimes b, [e_p] \boxtimes [e_{q,2}] \boxtimes b\}$$

$$K_1(C(S^1 \cup S^0, \mathcal{K})) \simeq \mathbb{Z} \qquad \{b\}$$

$$K_0(C_0(S^1 \times S^0 \times (0,\infty), \mathcal{K})) \simeq \mathbb{Z}^2 , \{b \boxtimes [e_{q,1}] \boxtimes b, b \boxtimes [e_{q,2}] \boxtimes b\} .$$

Reasoning as in Example 4.6, we have

$$\delta_0([e_p]) = [e_p] \boxtimes [e_{q,1}] \boxtimes b \oplus [e_p] \boxtimes [e_{q,2}] \boxtimes b$$

$$\delta_0([e_{q,i}]) = [e_p] \boxtimes [e_{q,i}] \boxtimes b , \qquad i=1,2$$

$$\delta_1(b) = b \boxtimes [e_{q,1}] \boxtimes b \oplus b \boxtimes [e_{q,2}] \boxtimes b .$$

Therefore, the element in $KK^1(C(S^1 \cup S^0, \mathcal{K}), C_0(S^1 \times S^0 \times (0,\infty), M_2(\mathcal{K})) \simeq \mathrm{Hom}(\mathbb{Z}^3, \mathbb{Z}^2) \oplus \mathrm{Hom}(\mathbb{Z}, \mathbb{Z}^2)$ represented by the extension (4.1) when $p=2$, $q=1$, is given by

$$(\delta_0, \delta_1) = \begin{pmatrix} 1 & 1 \\ 1 & 0 \\ 0 & 1 \end{pmatrix} \oplus \begin{pmatrix} 1 \\ 1 \end{pmatrix}$$

with respect to the bases above.

LEMMA 4.8. *In the following six term exact sequence (comparing with* (2.13)*) associated to the "deunitalized" short exact sequence* (2.11):

$$(4.25)\qquad \begin{array}{ccccc} K^0(S^{p-1}\cup S^{q-1}) & \xrightarrow{j^0_*} & K_0(B) & \longrightarrow & K^0(\mathbb{R}) \\ {\scriptstyle \mathrm{ind}}\uparrow & & & & \downarrow{\scriptstyle \exp} \\ K^1(\mathbb{R}) & \xleftarrow{\pi_{0,*}} & K_1(B) & \longleftarrow & K^1(S^{p-1}\cup S^{q-1}) \end{array}$$

both j^0_* *and* $\pi_{0,*}$ *are onto. Furthermore,* $K_1(B) \cong K^1(B) \oplus K^1(S^{p-1}\cup S^{q-1})$.

Proof. Because $K^0(\mathbb{R}) = 0$ and ind is injective (Proposition 2.4). Q.E.D.

THEOREM 4.9. *In the following six term exact sequence*

$$(4.26)\qquad \begin{array}{ccccc} K^0(S^{p-1}\times S^{q-1}\times \mathbb{R}) & \longrightarrow & K_0(C^*(G)) & \longrightarrow & K_0(B) \\ {\scriptstyle \bar{\delta}_1}\uparrow & & & & \downarrow{\scriptstyle \bar{\delta}_0} \\ K_1(B) & \xleftarrow{\pi_{x,*}} & K_1(C^*(G)) & \longleftarrow & K_1(S^{p-1}\times S^{q-1}\times \mathbb{R}) \end{array}$$

associated to the deunitalized short exact sequence (2.9), *both connecting maps* $\bar{\delta}_0$ *and* $\bar{\delta}_1$ *are determined by the connecting maps* δ_0 *and* δ_1 *of* (4.17) *(given in Corollaries 4.4, 4.5) via the commuting diagrams* (i=0,1):

$$\begin{array}{ccc} & \overset{j^i_*}{\nearrow} & K_i(B) \\ K^i(S^{p-1}\cup S^{q-1}) & & \downarrow{\scriptstyle \bar{\delta}_i} \\ & \underset{\delta_i}{\searrow} & K^{i+1}(S^{p-1}\times S^{q-1}\times \mathbb{R}) \end{array}$$

and the fact that

(1) j^0_* *is onto*

(2) $K_1(B) \cong K^1(\mathbb{R}) \oplus K^1(S^{p-1}\cup S^{q-1})$, *and* $\bar{\delta}_1\big|_{K^1(\mathbb{R})} = 0$.

<u>Proof</u>. By Lemma 4.8, it only need to show $\bar{\delta}_1\Big|_{K^1(\mathbb{R})} = 0$. This follows from the fact that the composite

$$K^1(\mathbb{R}) \simeq K_1(C(S^1)) \xleftarrow{\pi_{0,*}} K_1(B^+) \xleftarrow{\pi_{x,*}} K_1(C^*(p,q)^+)$$

is onto. Consider the generator $[1+g]$ of $K_1(C^*(p,q)^+)$ defined by (2.20), which maps to a generator $[1+\pi_0(g)]$ of $K_1(C_0(\mathbb{R}))$ (2.21) under the composite. Q.E.D.

<u>Example 4.11</u>. By Connes' isomorphism [Conn 1], $K_i(C^*(G(p,q))) = K_i(C_0(\mathbb{R}^{p+q}) \times \mathbb{R}) \cong K^{i+1}(\mathbb{R}^{p+q}) = 0$ if $p + q \equiv i (\mathrm{mod}\ 2)$ and $= 1$ if $p + 1 \equiv i + 1 \ (\mathrm{mod}\ 2)$. When $p = q = 1$, the six term exact sequence (4.26) reduces to

$$\begin{array}{ccccc}
0 & \longrightarrow & 0 & \longrightarrow & \mathbb{Z}^3 \\
\uparrow \bar{\delta}_1 & & & & \downarrow \bar{\delta}_0 \\
0 & \longleftarrow & \mathbb{Z} & \longleftarrow & \mathbb{Z}^4
\end{array}$$

So $\bar{\delta}_0$ is injective and $K^1(S^1 \times S^1 \times \mathbb{R})$ splits into direct sum of $K_0(B)$ and $K_1(C^*(G(1,1)))$.

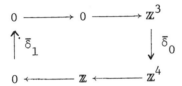

§5. THE STRUCTURE OF $C^*(G(p,q))$: THE MAIN THEOREMS

In §2; §3 and §4 we determined all the ideals and quotients of the $C^*(G(p,q))$ with respect to various decompositions (see (2.4)-(2.11)). In this section we shall assemble the parts produced in previous sections and describe explicitly the structure of the group C*-algebras $C^*(G(p,q))$. Among the crucial results obtained in previous sections are the structures of the quotient algebras B given in Theorem 2.5 (see (2.9)) and the structure of the C*-algebra $C^*(U,\mathcal{G})$ of the foliation given in Theorem 4.3 (see (2.4)). Although we determined the structures of the C*-algebras B constructively with respect to the $\mathbb{R}$-actions, we know only an isomorphic image $C^*(U,\mathcal{G})$ of the ideal $C_0(U) \rtimes_\sigma \mathbb{R}$. In order to use these results to study $C^*(G(p,q))$, we have to compute $C_0(U) \rtimes_\sigma \mathbb{R}$ with respect to the left Haar system arising from the given $\mathbb{R}$-action, or rather, to determine the isomorphism between $C^*(U,\mathcal{G})$ and $C_0(U) \rtimes_\sigma \mathbb{R}$. It will be necessary for us to go into much more detail.

Recall that we denote S_{PQ} to be the quarter plane with the boundary except the origin (Figure 4.1). Let $\dot{S}_{PQ}$ be the closed half plane and $\mathring{S}_{PQ}$ be its interior. We shall first study the transformation group C*-algebra $C_0(\dot{S}_{PQ}) \rtimes_\sigma \mathbb{R}$, where the $\mathbb{R}$-action on S_{PQ} is the restriction of the $\mathbb{R}$-action on $\hat{\mathbb{R}}^{p+q}$. We want to express $C_0(S_{PQ}) \rtimes \mathbb{R}$ as continuous fields of C*-algebras. Let $g \in C_c(\hat{\mathbb{R}}, C_c(\mathbb{R}^{p+q})) \subset C^*(G(p,q))$ be any element. Then the restriction of g naturally defines an element in $C_c(\mathbb{R}, C_c(\dot{S}_{PQ}))$. For simplicity we shall again denote the restriction of g by g. We shall assume that every element $g \in C_c(\mathbb{R}, C_c(\dot{S}_{PQ}))$ is obtained in this way without further explanation.

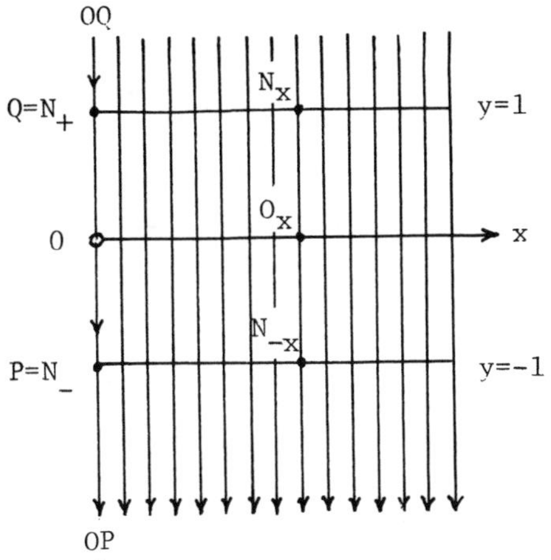

Figure 5.1

We use the closed half plane with origin deleted as the model for S_{PQ}; the $\mathbb{R}$-action induces vertical constant foliation. See Figure 5.1 above.

Let $N_x = (x,1)$, $N_{-x} = (x,-1)$, $0_x = (x,0)$ for every $x \geq 0$, and let $N_+ = (0,1)$ and $N_- = (0,-1)$. Note that the horizontal coordinate x corresponds exactly to the "diagonal transversal" coordinate γ which we used in the proof of Theorem 3.3. We do not need to know a specific $\mathbb{R}$-action σ, just assume that it is continuous, free, without loss of generality, and "symmetric", i.e. if $\sigma_t(x,y) = 0_x$ then $\sigma_{-t}(x,-y) = 0_x$ for all $t \in \mathbb{R}$, $(x,y) \in S_{pq}$. The reason for making this assumption is merely to reduce the notation.

Let $\ell_x > 0$ be given by $\sigma_{-\ell x}(0_x) = N_x$, $\sigma_{\ell x}(0_x) = N_{-x}$ for $x > 0$. Then by the continuity of σ, we see that ℓ_x is a continuous function of x. Since $\ell_0 = \infty$, so

(5.1)
$$\lim_{x \to 0^+} \ell_x = \infty \quad .$$

Therefore if we let

$$(5.2)\qquad \begin{aligned} P_x &= M_{\chi_{[-\ell_x,\infty)}} & Q_x &= I - P_x \\ Q_x &= M_{\chi_{(-\infty,\ell_x)}} & P_{-x} &= I - Q_{-x} \end{aligned}$$

then $P_x \nearrow I$, $Q_{-x} \nearrow I$ in $B(L^2(\mathbb{R}))$ with *-strong operator topology when $x \to 0^+$. Of course

$$P_{-x} \xrightarrow{*\text{-st}} 0 \ , \qquad Q_x \xrightarrow{*\text{-st}} 0$$

as $x \to 0^+$. However these are unitary equivalence relations between those projections:

$$(5.3)\qquad P_{-x} = U_x^* P_{-x} U_x \ , \qquad Q_x = U_x^* Q_{-x} U_x$$

where U_x is a translation operator on $L^2(\mathbb{R})$:

$$(5.4)\qquad (U_x\xi)(t) = \xi(t - 2\ell_x) \qquad t \in \mathbb{R} \ .$$

For any point $N \in S_{PQ}$, $S \in \mathbb{R}$, we simply denote $S \cdot N$ instead of $\sigma_{-S}(N)$ (*not* $\sigma_S(N)$*!*). There are three unitarily equivalent representations of $C_0(\dot{S}_{PQ}) \rtimes_\sigma \mathbb{R}$ for each $x > 0$:

$$(\pi_{N_x}(g)\xi)(S) = \int_{\mathbb{R}} g(S\cdot N_x, t)\xi(S-t)\,dt$$

$$(\pi_{N_{-x}}(g)\xi)(S) = \int_{\mathbb{R}} g(S\cdot N_{-x}, t)\xi(S-t)\,dt \qquad S \in \mathbb{R}$$

$$(\pi_{0_x}(g)\xi)(S) = \int_{\mathbb{R}} g(S\cdot 0_x, t)\xi(S-t)\,dt$$

where $g \in C_c(\mathbb{R}, C_c(\dot{S}_{PQ}))$, $\xi \in L^2(\mathbb{R})$.

Theorem 3.3 (iii) tells us that for any $g \in C_0(S_{PQ}) \rtimes_\sigma \mathbb{R} \subset C_0(\dot{S}_{PQ}) \rtimes_\sigma \mathbb{R}$, $\pi_{0_x}(g) \xrightarrow{*\text{-st}} 0$ as $x \to 0^+$. However the "amalgamated" representations which we now define will change all this dramatically.

To motivate our definition, we consider $\pi_{N_x}(g)$ and $\pi_{N_{-x}}(g)$ acting on two copies of Hilbert spaces, $L^2(G_x)$ and $L^2(G_{-x})$, although in (5.5) they act simply on $L^2(\mathbb{R})$. (This is apparent in the context of foliations; see (2.5).)

For every $g \in C_0(\dot{S}_{PQ}) \rtimes \mathbb{R}$ and $x > 0$, let

$$\text{(5.6)} \qquad \begin{aligned} \pi^x_{11}(g) &= P_x \pi_{N_x}(g) P_x & \qquad \pi^x_{12}(g) &= P_{-x} \pi_{N_{-x}}(g) Q_{-x} \\ \pi^x_{21}(g) &= Q_x \pi_{N_x}(g) P_x & \qquad \pi^x_{22}(g) &= Q_{-x} \pi_{N_{-x}}(g) Q_{-x} \end{aligned}$$

Their domains and ranges are shown below:

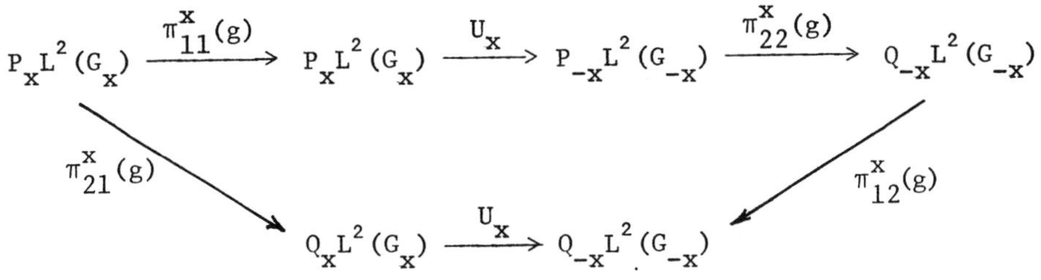

Recall (5.3) and (5.4) for the vertical unitary operator. Put the diagram slightly different:

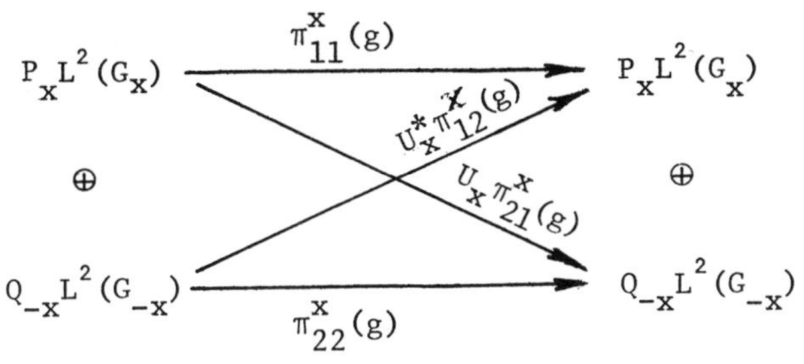

Now we define $\hat{\pi}_x(g) \in B(P_x L^2(\mathbb{R}) \oplus Q_{-x} L^2(\mathbb{R})) \subset B(L^2(\mathbb{R}) \oplus L^2(\mathbb{R}))$ by

$$(5.7)\qquad \hat{\pi}_x(g) = \begin{pmatrix} \pi_{11}^x(g) & U_x^*\pi_{12}^x(g) \\ U_x\pi_{21}^x(g) & \pi_{22}^x(g) \end{pmatrix}$$

where the entries are in $B(L^2(\mathbb{R}))$ and given by (5.4), (5.5) and (5.6).

In addition to (5.3), it is easily seen that

$$(5.8)\qquad \pi_{N_x}(g) = U_x^* \pi_{N_{-x}}(g) U_x \quad .$$

Substitute (5.6) into (5.7), by (5.3) and (5.8) we get

$$(5.9)\qquad \hat{\pi}_x(g) = \begin{pmatrix} P_x\pi_{N_x}(g)P_x & P_x\pi_{N_x}(g)Q_xU_x^* \\ U_xQ_x\pi_{N_x}(g)P_x & U_xQ_x\pi_{N_x}(g)Q_xU_x^* \end{pmatrix} \quad .$$

Now for every $g \in C_c(\mathbb{R}, C_c(\dot{S}_{PQ}))$ we define $(\hat{\psi}_{PQ}g)(x) = \hat{\pi}_x(g)$ for all $x \in (0,\infty)$. Let $\bar{A}'$ be the (non-separable) C*-algebra for all the bounded norm continuous functions

$$(5.10)\qquad f\colon [0,\infty) \to \mathcal{K}(P_xL^2(\mathbb{R}) \oplus Q_{-x}L^2(\mathbb{R})) \subset \mathcal{K}(L^2(\mathbb{R}) \oplus L^2(\mathbb{R}))$$

such that

$$(5.11)\qquad f(x) \to 0 \text{ in norm when } x \to \infty \quad ,$$

$$(5.12)\qquad f(x) \xrightarrow{*\text{-st}} \begin{pmatrix} f_1 & 0 \\ 0 & f_2 \end{pmatrix} \text{ when } x \to 0 \,.$$

where $(f_1,f_2) \in C^*((S^*-I) \oplus 0) \oplus C^*(0 \oplus (S-I))$ and $\pi(f_1) = \pi(f_2)$ (cf. Proposition 3.2 and (2.37)).

LEMMA 5.1. *The mapping* $\hat{\psi}_{PQ}$ *extends to a natural imbedding of* $C_0(\dot{S}_{PQ}) \rtimes_\sigma \mathbb{R}$ *into* $\bar{A}'$ *such that if* $f = \hat{\psi}_{PQ} g$ *then* $(f_1, f_2) = (\pi_{N_+}(g), \pi_{N_-}(g))$. *(See the notation after Figure 5.1.)*

Proof. A straightforward computation now shows $\hat{\pi}_x(g_1 g_2) = \hat{\pi}_x(g_1)\hat{\pi}_x(g_2)$ and $\hat{\pi}_x$ is a *-representation of $C_0(\dot{S}_{PQ}) \rtimes_\sigma \mathbb{R}$

One can verify that the mapping $\hat{\psi}_{PQ} g\colon x \mapsto \hat{\pi}_x(g)$ is a norm continuous function from $(0,\infty)$ to $\mathcal{K}(L^2(\mathbb{R}) \oplus L^2(\mathbb{R}))$ for every $g \in C_0(\dot{S}_{PQ}) \rtimes_\sigma \mathbb{R}$. To check this, one need only apply Lemma 3.1 and make some triangle estimate to each entry in the matrix of (5.9). For instance, we have

$$\| P_x \pi_{N_x}(g) P_x - P_{x'} \pi_{N_{x'}}(g) P_{x'} \|$$

$$\leq \| P_x \pi_{N_x}(g) P_x - P_{x'} \pi_{N_x}(g) P_x \| + \| P_{x'} \pi_{N_x}(g) P_x - P_{x'} \pi_{N_x}(g) P_{x'} \|$$

$$+ \| P_{x'} \pi_{N_x}(g) P_{x'} - P_{x'} \pi_{N_{x'}}(g) P_{x'} \| \leq 3\varepsilon$$

when x' closes to x. We leave out the routine calculations.

It is also clear from Corollary 3.2 that the mapping $g \mapsto \hat{\psi}_{PQ}(g)$ defines an imbedding of $C_0(S_{PQ}) \rtimes \mathbb{R}$ into $C^b((0,\infty), \mathcal{K}(L^2(\mathbb{R}) + (L^2(\mathbb{R})))$. In fact, $\hat{\psi}_{PQ}(g) = 0$ implies

$$\begin{pmatrix} P_x \pi_{N_x}(g) P_x & P_x \pi_{N_x}(g) Q_x \\ Q_x \pi_{N_x}(g) P_x & Q_x \pi_{N_x}(g) Q_x \end{pmatrix} = 0 \quad \text{for all} \quad x \in (0,\infty) .$$

This is a decomposition of $\pi_{N_x}(g)$ over range $P_x \oplus$ range Q_x; see (5.2). Thus $\pi_{N_x}(g) = 0$ and therefore $\pi_{0_x}(g) = 0$; see the comments before (5.5).

Thus $\psi g = \{x \mapsto \pi_{0_x}(g)\} = 0$, and $g=0$ (Corollary 3.2). We conclude that $\hat{\psi}_{PQ}$ imbeds $C_0(\dot{S}_{PQ}) \rtimes_\sigma \mathbb{R}$ into the C*-algebra of bounded norm continuous functions f satisfying (5.10) and vanishing at ∞.

Now we verify (5.12). First we show that for any $\xi \in L^2(\mathbb{R})$,

(5.13) $$\|P_x(\pi_{N_x}(g) - \pi_{N_+}(g))P_x\xi\| \longrightarrow 0 .$$

We actually have

(5.14) $$\pi_{N_x}(g) \xrightarrow{*\text{-st}} \pi_{N_+}(g)$$

i.e. for $\xi \in L^2(\mathbb{R})$, that

(5.15) $$\|(\pi_{N_x}(g) - \pi_{N_+}(g))\xi\| \to 0$$

for any $g \in C_0(\dot{S}_{PQ}) \rtimes \mathbb{R}$. Note $\pi_{N_x}(g)^* - \pi_{N_+}(g)^* = \pi_{N_x}(g^*) - \pi_{N_+}(g^*)$ so *-strong convergence follows from (5.15).

We don't need (5.14) at this moment and the proof of (5.15) is similar to that of (5.13), so let's do (5.13) directly. Suppose we have shown (5.13) is true for all $g \in C_c(\mathbb{R}, C_c(\dot{S}_{PQ}))$. For any $g_1 \in C_0(\dot{S}_{PQ}) \rtimes \mathbb{R}$, given $\varepsilon > 0$, pick $g \in C_c(\mathbb{R}, C_c(\dot{S}_{PQ}))$ such that $\|g - g_1\| < \varepsilon$ then

$$\|P_x(\pi_{N_x}(g_1) - \pi_{N_+}(g_1))P_x\xi\|$$

$$\leq \|P_x(\pi_{N_x}(g_1) - \pi_{N_x}(g))P_x\xi\| \quad \|P_x(\pi_{N_x}(g) - \pi_{N_+}(g))P_x\xi\|$$

$$+ \|P_x(\pi_{N_+}(g) - \pi_{N_+}(g_1))P_x\xi\| \leq 3\varepsilon$$

when x small enough. (We will not repeat this routine 3-ε estimate anymore.) Thus (5.13) is true for all $g \in C_0(\dot{S}_{PQ}) \rtimes \mathbb{R}$.

Therefore we may assume $g \in C_c(\mathbb{R}, C_c(\dot{S}_{PQ}))$. A straightforward computation shows

$$(5.16) \qquad P_x \pi_{N_x}(g) P_x \xi(s) = \chi_{(-\ell_x,\infty)} \int_{\mathbb{R}} g(s\cdot N_x, t)\chi_{(-\ell_x,\infty)}(s-t)\xi(s-t)dt .$$

A similar expression holds for π_{N_+}. Since $\|P_x(\pi_{N_x}(g) - \pi_{N_+}(g))P_x\| \leq 2\|g\|$, we may assume $\xi \in C_c(\mathbb{R})$. So let $\mathrm{supp}(g) \subseteq B_0(N)$ and $\mathrm{supp}(\xi) \subseteq B_0(N_1)$. One computes

$$\|P_x(\pi_{N_x}(g) - \pi_{N_+}(g))P_x\xi\|^2$$

$$= \int_{\ell}^{\infty} \left| \int_{\mathbb{R}} (g(s\cdot N_x,t) - g(s\cdot N_+,t))\chi_{(-\ell_x,\infty)}(s-t)\xi(s-t)dt \right|^2 dt$$

$$(5.17) \qquad = \int_{-\ell_x}^{\infty} \left| \int_{-\ell_x}^{\infty} (g(s\cdot N_x,s-t) - g(s\cdot N_+,s-t))\xi(t)dt \right|^2 ds$$

$$= \int_{-N_1-N}^{N_1+N} \left| \int_{-N_1}^{N_1} (g(s\cdot N_x,s-t) - g(s\cdot N_+,s-t))\xi(t)dt \right|^2 ds$$

Given any $\varepsilon > 0$ there is $\delta > 0$ such that

$$|g(x,t) - g(y,t)| < \varepsilon$$

if $|x-y| < \delta$, all $t \in \mathbb{R}$. Since the $\mathbb{R}$-action is continuous, there is $\delta' > 0$ such that when $0 \leq x \leq \delta'$ we have $|s\cdot N_x - s\cdot N_+| < \delta$ for $s \in [-N_1N, N_1+N]$ and therefore expression (5.16) is less than $2(N_1+N)\cdot(2N_1)^2 \cdot \varepsilon^2 \cdot \|\xi\|_2^2$ so (5.13) holds. The proof is the same for

$$(5.18) \qquad \|Q_{-x}(\pi_{N_{-x}}(g) - \pi_{N_-}(g))Q_{-x}\xi\| \to 0$$

see (5.6) and (5.7).

We now verify that

(5.19) $$\|P_x \pi_{N_x}(g) Q_x U_x^* \xi\| \to 0 \ .$$

By a simple computation,

$$P_x \pi_{N_x}(g) Q_x U_x^* \xi(s)$$

$$= \chi_{(-\ell_x,\infty)}(s) \int_{\mathbb{R}} g(s\cdot N_x, t)\chi_{(-\infty,-\ell_x)}(s-t)\, \xi(s-t+2\ell_x)\,dt$$

$$= \chi_{(-\ell_x,\infty)}(s) \int_{-\infty}^{-\ell_x} g(s\cdot N_x, s-t)\xi(t+2\ell_x)\,dt$$

$$= \chi_{(-\ell_x,\infty)}(s) \int_{-2\ell_x-N}^{-2\ell_x+N} g(s\cdot N_x, s-t)\xi(t+2\ell_x)\,dt$$

when x is small and ℓ_x large enough.

(5.20) $$\|P_x \pi_{N_x}(g) Q_x U_x^* \xi\|^2$$

$$= \int_{-\ell_x}^{\infty} \left| \int_{-2\ell_x-N}^{-2\ell_x+N} g(s\cdot N_x, s-t)\xi(t+2\ell_x)\,dt \right|^2 ds \ .$$

Choose $\delta' > 0$ small such that if $0 \le x \le \delta'$, then $\ell_x > 2N$, so $-\ell_x - N > -2\ell_x + N$

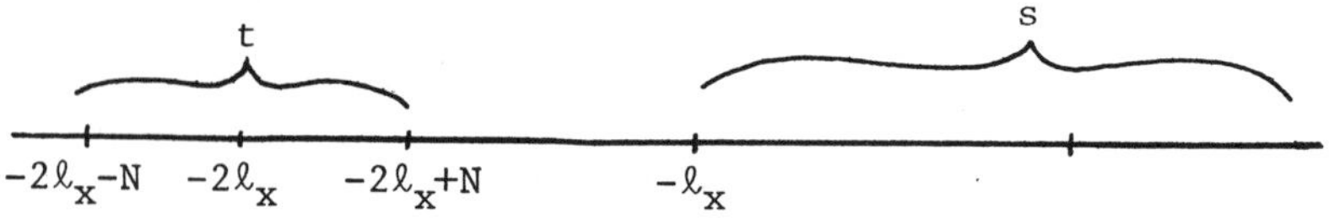

so $|s-t| > N$ if $s \in (-\ell_x,\infty)$ and $t \in (2\ell_x-N, -2\ell_x+N)$. So $g(s\cdot N_x, s-t) = 0$ for all s,t if $0 \le x \le \delta'$, so the expression (5.20) is equal to 0.

The proof for

$$\|U_x Q_x \pi_{N_x}(g) P_x \xi\| \to 0 \quad \text{if} \quad x \to 0$$

is similar and we omit it.

We have shown that

$$\hat{\psi}_{PQ} g^{\bullet}(x) - \begin{pmatrix} P_x \pi_{N_+}(g) P_x & 0 \\ 0 & Q_{-x} \pi_{N_-}(g) Q_{-x} \end{pmatrix} \xrightarrow{*-st} 0 \quad \text{when } x \to 0 .$$

By (5.12),

$$(5.21) \qquad \hat{\psi}_{PQ} g\ (x) \xrightarrow{*-st} \begin{pmatrix} \pi_{N_+}(g) & 0 \\ 0 & \pi_{N_-}(g) \end{pmatrix} \qquad \text{when } x \to 0 .$$

By Theorem 2.5 and its proof, we see that with the orthonormal basis (2.28) and (2.29) for $L^2(\mathbb{R})$,

$$\pi_{N_+}(g) \in C^*((S^* - I) \oplus 0) , \qquad \pi_{N_-}(g) \in C^*(0 \oplus (S - I))$$

with

$$\pi(\pi_{N_+}(g)) = \overline{\pi(\pi_{N_-}(g))} \in C_0(\mathbb{R}) .$$

Also see (2.26). Here again π is the Calkin map. This concludes the proof of Lemma 5.1. Q.E.D.

LEMMA 5.2. *Let* A' *be the separable* C^**-subalgebra of* $\overline{A'}$ *consisting of all* $f \in \overline{A'}$ *such that* $f(x) \to \text{diag}(f_1, f_2)$ *in norm when* $x \to 0$ (5.12). *Then the restriction of* ψ_{PQ} *on* $C_0(S_{PQ}) \rtimes \mathbb{R}$ *is an isomorphism onto* A'.

Proof. It suffices to show that for every $g \in C_0(S_{PQ}) \rtimes \mathbb{R}$,

$$(5.22)\qquad \hat{\pi}_x(g) = \begin{pmatrix} P_x\pi_{N_x}(g)P_x & P_x\pi_{N_x}(g)Q_xU_x^* \\ U_xQ_x\pi_{N_x}(g)P_x & U_xQ_x\pi_{N_x}(g)Q_xU_x^* \end{pmatrix} \longrightarrow \begin{pmatrix} \pi_{N_+}(g) & 0 \\ 0 & \pi_{N_-}(g) \end{pmatrix}$$

in norm when $x \to 0$ (Figure 5.1). By Theorem 2.5, $\pi_{N_+}(g), \pi_{N_-}(g) \in \mathcal{K}(L^2(\mathbb{R}))$. We begin by showing

$$(5.23)\qquad \|P_x(\pi_{N_x}(g) - \pi_{N_+}(g))P_x\| \longrightarrow 0 \quad .$$

It suffices to show this for all $g \in C_c(\mathbb{R}, C_c(S_{PQ}))$. Recall (5.16). A computation similar to (5.17) gives

$$(5.24)\qquad \|P_x(\pi_{N_x}(g) - \pi_{N_+}(g))P_x\|^2 \leq \int_{-\ell_x}^{\infty}\int_{-\ell_x}^{\infty} |g(s\cdot N_x, s-t) - g(s\cdot N_+, s-t)|^2 \, dt\, ds \quad .$$

Therefore,

$$(5.25)\qquad \|P_x(\pi_{N_x}(g) - \pi_{N_+}(g))P_x\| \leq \int_{-\ell_x}^{\infty}\int_{-\ell_x}^{\infty} |g(s\cdot N_x, s-t) - g(s\cdot N_+, s-t)|^2 \, dtds$$

$$\overset{s-t/\!/t}{=} \int_{-\ell_x}^{\infty}\int_{-\infty}^{s+\ell_x} |g(s\cdot N_x, t) - g(s\cdot N_+, t)|^2 \, dtds \quad .$$

We may assume that

(1) $\operatorname{supp}(g) \subset B_0(N)$ and

(2) $g(p,t) = 0$ for all $t \in \mathbb{R}$ if $|P| < \delta_0$.

By the continuity of the $\mathbb{R}$-action σ, there is a large $L_N > 0$ such that when $s > \ell_N$ then $|s\cdot N_+| > N$, $|s\cdot N_x| > N$ for all $0 \leq x \leq \delta_0/2$. Also there is a large L_{δ_0} such that if $s \in (-\ell_x, -L_{\delta_0})$ then $|s\cdot N_x| < \delta_0$ for $0 \leq x \leq \delta_0/2$ and $|s\cdot N_+| < \delta_0$. By the assumption on g the expressions in (5.25) becomes

$$(5.25') \qquad \int_{-L_{\delta_0}}^{L_N} \int_{-N}^{N} |g(s\cdot N_x, t) - g(s\cdot N_+, t)|^2 \, dtds$$

Now because $g \in C_c(\mathbb{R}, C_c(S_{PQ}))$, for given $\varepsilon > 0$, there exists $\delta > 0$ such that when $|M - M'| < \delta$

$$|g(M,t) - g(M' - t)| < \varepsilon \qquad \text{for all} \quad t \in \mathbb{R} .$$

Choose small $\delta' > 0$ so that when $0 \leq x \leq \delta'$, we have $|s\cdot N_x - s\cdot N_+| < \delta$ for all $s \in (-L_{\delta_0}, L_N)$. Then for any x, $0 \leq x \leq \min\{\delta_0/2, \delta'\}$, we have by (5.25')

$$\|P_x(\pi_{N_x}(g) - \pi_{N_+}(g))P_x\| \leq (L_N + L_{\delta_0}) \cdot 2N \cdot \varepsilon^2$$

This proves (5.25).

We show next under the same assumption on g that

$$(5.26) \qquad \|P_x \pi_{N_x}(g) Q_x\| \longrightarrow 0 \qquad \text{as} \qquad x \longrightarrow 0 \ .$$

A straight computation as before shows

$$(5.27) \qquad \|P_x \pi_{N_x}(g) Q_x\|^2 \leq \int_{-\ell_x}^{\infty} \int_{-\infty}^{-\ell_x} |g(s\cdot N_x, s-t)|^2 \, dtds$$

$$\overset{s-t/\!/t}{=} \int_{-\ell_x}^{\infty} \int_{s+\ell_x}^{\infty} |g(s\cdot N_x, t)|^2 \, dtds$$

$$= \int_{-\ell_x}^{-\ell_x+N} \int_{s+\ell_x}^{N} |g(s\cdot N_x, t)|^2 \, dtds$$

(the last equality is by assumption on g, and that $N \geq s+\ell_x$).
By the continuity of σ, we define a function q on $[0,\infty)$ by

$$(x,\ q(x)) = N\cdot(x,0)\ , \qquad x \in (0,\infty)\ ,$$

then q is a positive continuous function; see Figure 5.2.

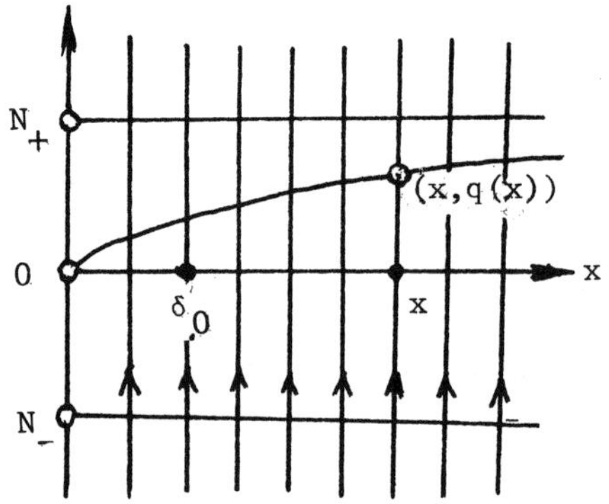

Figure 5.2

Since $q(0)=0$, 0 is fixed by σ, and naturally $\lim_{x\to 0} q(x) = 0$.
Choose $\delta' > 0$ such that

1) $0 \leq x < \delta'$ implies that $q(x) < \delta_0/2$

2) $\delta' < \delta_0/2$.

Then when $0 \leq x < \delta'$, $s \in (-\ell_x, -\ell_x+N)$, we have

$$|s\cdot N_x| \leq |(-\ell_x+N)\cdot N_x| = |(x,q)(x))| < \frac{\delta_0}{2} + \frac{\delta_0}{2} = \delta_0\ .$$

It follows from the assumption on g that $g(s\cdot N_x,t) = 0$. From (5.27) we see that

$$\|P_x\pi_{N_x}(g)Q_x\| = 0 \qquad \text{when} \qquad 0 \leq x < \delta'\ .$$

Take conjugation on (5.26), one gets

$$\|Q_x\pi_{N_x}(g)P_x\| \to 0 \quad \text{as} \quad x \to 0 \tag{5.28}$$

for any $g \in C_0(S_{PQ}) \rtimes \mathbb{R}$.

By triangle estimate, recall that $\pi_{N_+}(g)$ is compact and $\{P_x\}$ is an approximate identity for compacts, and we conclude from (5.23) that

$$(5.29) \qquad \| P_x \pi_{N_x}(g) P_x - \pi_{N_+}(g) \| \to 0 \quad \text{as} \quad x \to 0 .$$

By symmetry,

$$(5.30) \qquad \| Q_{-x} \pi_{N_{-x}}(g) Q_{-x} - \pi_{N_-}(g) \| \to 0 \quad \text{as} \quad x \to 0 .$$

This finishes the proof of (5.22).

So far we have proved that $\hat{\psi}$ identifies $C_0(S_{PQ}) \rtimes_\sigma \mathbb{R}$ with a C*-subalgebra B of A'. It remains to show that B = A'. There are several ways to see this. A simple one is to show that B is a rich sub-C*-algebra of A' ([Dix], 11.1.1) and then apply Proposition 11.1.6 [Dix].

It is clear that N_+ and N_- give rise to irreducible representations of both A and B. From (5.9) we actually have $\hat{\pi}_x$ and π_{N_x} unitarily equivalent, because

$$(5.31) \qquad \hat{\pi}_x(g) = \begin{pmatrix} 1 & 0 \\ 0 & U_x \end{pmatrix} \begin{pmatrix} P_x N_x(g) P_x & P_x N_x(g) Q_x \\ Q_x N_x(g) P_x & Q_x N_x(g) Q_x \end{pmatrix} \begin{pmatrix} 1 & 0 \\ 0 & U_x^* \end{pmatrix} \qquad x > 0$$

so that $\hat{\pi}_x$ is an irreducible representation for both A' and B, and $\hat{\pi}_x \not\simeq \hat{\pi}_{x'}$ if $x \neq x'$. It follows that B is a rich C*-subalgebra of A'.

Q.E.D.

The following is now obvious from the proof of Lemma 5.2.

COROLLARY 5.3. *With the notation of Lemma 5.2, let*

$$\mathring{A}' = \{f \in A' \mid \text{corresponding to } f_1, f_2 = 0\} \quad . \tag{5.32}$$

Then $\mathring{A}'$ *is an ideal of* A' *and the following canonical exact sequences commutes:*

$$\begin{array}{ccccccccc} 0 & \longrightarrow & \mathring{A}' & \longrightarrow & A' & \xrightarrow{\pi'_{PQ}} & \mathcal{K}(L^2(\mathbb{R}))^2 & \longrightarrow & 0 \\ & & \uparrow \simeq \; \hat{\psi}_{PQ}|_{C^*(\dot{S}_{PQ},\mathcal{G})} & & \uparrow \simeq \; \hat{\psi}_{PQ} & & \uparrow \simeq & & \\ 0 & \longrightarrow & C_0(\mathring{S}_{PQ}) \rtimes \mathbb{R} & \longrightarrow & C_0(S_{PQ}) \rtimes \mathbb{R} & \xrightarrow{\pi_{PQ}} & C_0(\partial S_{PQ}) \rtimes \mathbb{R} & \longrightarrow & 0 \end{array} \tag{5.33}$$

where $\pi'_{PQ}(f) = (f_1, f_2)$.

With respect to the left Haar system induced by the $\mathbb{R}$-action, we obtain a description $C_0(S_{PQ}) \rtimes \mathbb{R}$ which depends on the projection system $\{P_x\}$ and $\{Q_x\}$ in Lemmas 5.1 and 5.2. We have pointed out that $C_0(S_{PQ}) \rtimes \mathbb{R}$ is isomorphic to the C*-algebra $C^*(S_{PQ}, \mathcal{G})$ with another left Haar system induced from foliation and whose structure can be explicitly described by Theorem 4.3. In order to obtain the structure of $C_0(\dot{S}_{PQ}) \rtimes \mathbb{R}$, we shall find this isomorphism explicitly. For the following lemma, see 10.8.1 and 10.8.7 of [Dix].

LEMMA 5.4. *The continuous field of Hilbert spaces* $\{P_x L^2(\mathbb{R}) \oplus Q_{-x} L^2(\mathbb{R})\}_{x \geq 0}$ *is trivial. More precisely, there exists a family of partial isometries*

$$V_x = V_x^+ \oplus V_x^- : P_x L^2(\mathbb{R}) \oplus Q_{-x} L^2(\mathbb{R}) \xrightarrow{\simeq} L^2(\mathbb{R}) \oplus L^2(\mathbb{R}) \quad (x \geq 0) \tag{5.34}$$

such that

1) $V_0 = I$,

2) *The mapping* $x \to V_x \begin{pmatrix} P_x & 0 \\ 0 & Q_{-x} \end{pmatrix}$, $x \in [0,\infty)$ *is continuous in the *-strong topology of* $B(L^2(\mathbb{R}) + L^2(\mathbb{R}))$.

Proof. Recall (5.2).

$$P_x L^2(\mathbb{R}) = L^2(-\ell_x, \infty) , \qquad Q_{-x} L^2(\mathbb{R}) = L^2(-\infty, \ell_x) .$$

For $\xi \in L^2(-\ell_x, \infty)$, $\eta \in L^2(-\infty, \ell_x)$, we define $V_x^+\xi, V_x^-\eta \in L^2(\mathbb{R})$, $x > 0$ by

$$\text{(5.35)} \qquad V_x^+\xi(t) = \begin{cases} \xi(t) & \text{if } t \geq -\ell_x + 1 \\ \dfrac{1}{t - 2 + \ell_x}\, \xi\left(-\ell_x - \dfrac{1}{t-2+\ell_x}\right) & \text{if } t < -\ell_x + 1 , \end{cases}$$

$$\text{(5.36)} \qquad V_x^-\eta(t) = \begin{cases} \dfrac{1}{t + 2 - \ell_x}\, \eta\left(\ell_x - \dfrac{1}{t+2-\ell_x}\right) & \text{if } t > \ell_x - 1 \\ \eta(t) & \text{if } t \leq \ell_x - 1 . \end{cases}$$

Then

$$\|V_x^+\xi\|^2 = \int_{-\infty}^{-\ell_{x+1}} \frac{1}{(t - 2 + \ell_x)^2} \left|\xi\left(-\ell_x - \frac{1}{t-2+\ell_x}\right)\right|^2 dt + \int_{-\ell_{x+1}}^{\infty} |\xi(t)|^2\, dt$$

$$= \int_{-\ell_x}^{\ell_{x+1}} |\xi(t)|^2\, dt + \int_{-\ell_{x+1}}^{\infty} |\xi(t)|^2\, dt = \|\xi\|^2$$

Similarly, $\|V_x^-\eta\|^2 = \|\eta\|^2$.

It is easy to see that V_x is onto. Its inverse is given by (for $\xi, \eta \in L^2(\mathbb{R})$),

$$(5.37) \qquad V_x^{-1^+}\xi(t) = \begin{cases} \xi(t) & \text{if} \quad t \geq -\ell_x+1 \\ \dfrac{1}{t+\ell_x}\,\xi\!\left(2-\ell_x-\dfrac{1}{t+\ell_x}\right) & \text{if} \quad -\ell_x < t < -\ell_x+1 \end{cases}$$

$$(5.38) \qquad V_x^{-1^-}\eta(t) = \begin{cases} \dfrac{1}{\ell_x - t}\,\eta\!\left(\ell_x-2+\dfrac{1}{\ell_x-t}\right) & \text{if} \quad \ell_x-1 < t < \ell_x \\ \eta(t) & \text{if} \quad t \leq \ell_x-1 \end{cases}$$

The homeomorphisms $(-\ell_x,\infty) \approx (-\infty,\infty)$, $(-\infty,\ell_x) \approx (-\infty,\infty)$ are illustrated below.

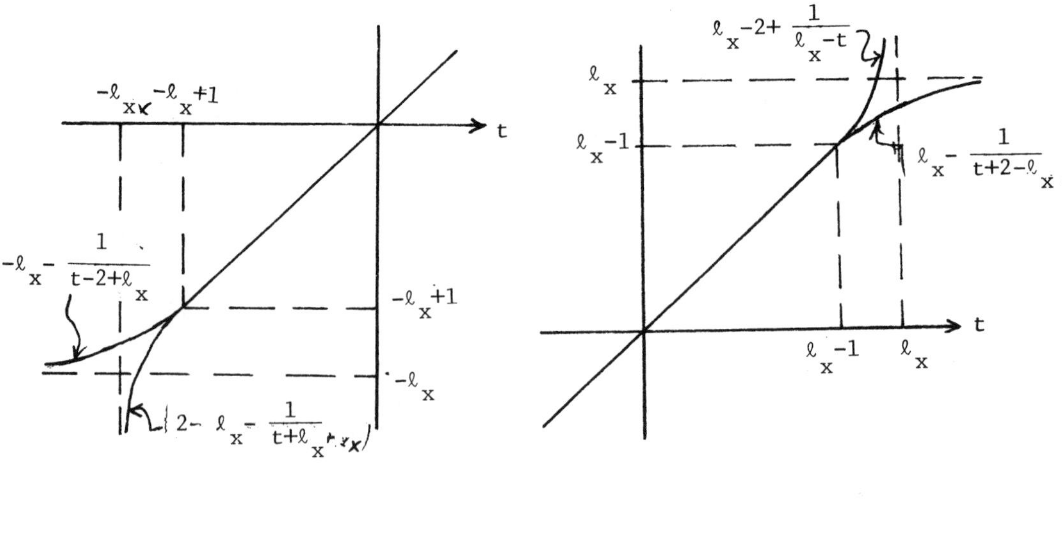

Figure 5.3

Consider $$L^2(\mathbb{R}) \underset{P_x V_x^{+*}}{\overset{V_x^+ P_x}{\rightleftarrows}} L^2(\mathbb{R}) \quad .$$

We claim that

a) $x \mapsto V_x^+ P_x$ is strong continous, $x \in (0,\infty)$

b) $V_x^+ P_x \xrightarrow{\text{st.}} I$ when $x \to 0$

c) $x \mapsto P_x V_x^{+*} = V_x^{+-1}$ is strong continuous, $x \in (0,\infty)$

d) $V_x^{+-1} \xrightarrow{\text{st.}} I$ when $x \to 0$.

Once these are verified, there will be similar conclusions for $\bar{V}_x Q_{-x}$ and (2) will follow.

We begin with (c); suppose $0 < x < x'$ (if $0 < x' < x$, the discussion is similar), and x' is already close enough to x, so by continuity of ℓ , we have

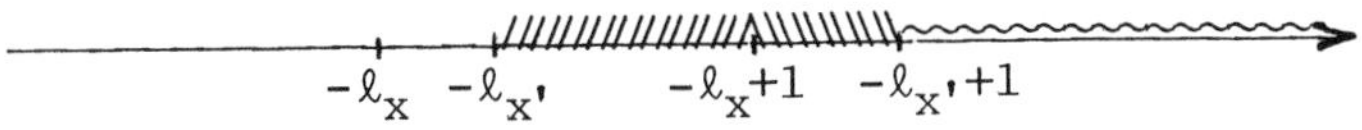

Figure 5.4

We need only consider an arbitrary $\xi \in C_c(\mathbb{R}) \subset L^2(\mathbb{R})$, because the norm of $V_x^+ P_x$ is bounded by 1.

$$\| V_x^{-1} - V_{x'}^{-1}\xi \|^2 = 2\|\xi\|^2 - 2\mathrm{Re}\langle V_x^{-1}\xi, V_{x'}^{-1}\xi\rangle$$

$$= 2\|\xi\|^2 - 2\mathrm{Re}\int_{-\ell_x}^{-\ell_x+1} \frac{1}{(t+\ell_x)(t+\ell_{x'})}\, \xi\left(2-\ell_x-\frac{1}{t+\ell_x}\right)\bar{\xi}\left(2-\ell_x-\frac{1}{t+\ell_{x'}}\right)dt$$

$$- 2\mathrm{Re}\int_{-\ell_x+1}^{-\ell_{x'}+1} \frac{1}{t+\ell_{x'}}\, \xi\left(2-\ell_{x'}-\frac{1}{t+\ell_{x'}}\right)\bar{\xi}(t)dt - 2\int_{-\ell_{x'}+1}^{\infty} |\xi(t)|^2\, dt$$

(5.39)

Assume that $\sup_{t\in\mathbb{R}} |\xi(t)| = M$ and $\text{supp}(\xi) \subseteq B_0(N-2-2\ell_x)$. Then

$$\frac{1}{t+\ell_x} > N \implies \xi(2-\ell_x - \frac{1}{t+\ell_x}) = 0$$

so the integrand of the first integral in (5.39) is bounded by N^2M^2. It is clear by Lebesgue's bounded convergence theorem that when $x' \to x$, $\ell_{x'} \to \ell_x$ the first integral converges to

$$-2\text{Re}\int_{\ell_x}^{\ell_x+1} \frac{1}{(t+\ell_x)^2} |\xi(2-\ell_x - \frac{1}{t+\ell_x})|^2 \, dt = -2\int_{-\infty}^{\ell_x+1} |\xi(t)|^2 \, dt$$

and that the second integral in (5.39) converges to 0 and that the third integral converges to $-2\int_{-\ell_x}^{\infty} |\xi(t)|^2 \, dt$. Thus the expression (5.39) converges to 0 when $x' \to x$.

For (d) we compute by (5.37),

$$\begin{aligned}
\|V_x^{+-1}\xi - \xi\|^2 &= \int_{-\infty}^{-\ell_x+1} |V_x^{+-1}\xi(t) - \xi(t)|^2 \, dt \\
&\leq 2\int_{-\ell_x}^{-\ell_x+1} |V_x^{+-1}\xi(t)|^2 \, dt + 2\int_{-\infty}^{-\ell_x+1} |\xi(t)|^2 \, dt \\
&= 4\int_{-\infty}^{\ell_x+1} |\xi(t)|^2 \, dt \to 0 \quad \text{as} \quad x \to 0 .
\end{aligned}$$

For (b) we have (see (5.35)),

$$\begin{aligned}
\|V_x^+P_x\xi - \xi\|^2 &\leq \int_{-\infty}^{\ell_x+1} |V_x^+P_x\xi(t) - \xi(t)|^2 \, dt \\
&\leq 2\int_{\infty}^{-\ell_x+1} |V_x^+P_x\xi(t)|^2 \, dt + 2\int^{\ell_x+1} |\xi(t)|^2 \, dt \\
&= 2\int_{-\ell_x}^{-\ell_x+1} |\xi(t)|^2 \, dt + 2\int_{-\infty}^{-\ell_x+1} |\xi(t)|^2 \, dt \to 0
\end{aligned}$$

when $x \to 0$ and $\ell_x \to \infty$.

For (a) we have (see (5.35) and Figure 5.4),

$$(5.40) \quad \| V_x^+ P_x \xi - V_{x'}^+ P_{x'} \xi \|^2$$

$$= \|P_x \xi\|^2 + \|P_{x'}\xi\|^2 - 2\mathrm{Re}\,\langle V_x^+ P_x \xi,\ V_{x'}^+ P_{x'} \xi\rangle$$

$$= \|P_x \xi\|^2 + \|P_{x'}\xi\|^2$$

$$- 2\mathrm{Re} \int_{-\infty}^{-\ell_x+1} \frac{1}{(t-2+\ell_x)} \frac{1}{(t-2+\ell_{x'})} \xi(-\ell_x - \frac{1}{t-2+\ell_x}) \bar{\xi}(-\ell_{x'} - \frac{1}{t-2+\ell_{x'}}) dt$$

$$- 2\mathrm{Re} \int_{-\ell_x+1}^{-\ell_x+1} \frac{1}{t-2+\ell_{x'}} \xi(t) \bar{\xi}(-\ell_{x'} - \frac{1}{t-2+\ell_{x'}}) dt - 2 \int_{-\ell_x+1}^{\infty} |\xi(t)|^2 dt$$

Since $\sup|\xi| = M < \infty$, the integrand of the first integral is bounded by $\dfrac{M^2}{(t - 3/2 + \ell_x)^2}$ when $\ell_{x'} \to \ell_x$. Apply Lebesgue's controlled convergence theorem, and the first integral converges to

$$\int_{-\infty}^{\ell_x+1} \frac{1}{(t-2+\ell_x)^2} \left|\xi(-\ell_x - \frac{1}{t-2+\ell_x})\right|^2 dt = -2 \int_{-\ell_x}^{-\ell_x+1} |\xi(t)|^2 dt \quad \text{as } x' \to x .$$

The second integral in (5.40) converges to 0, and the third integral converges to

$$-2 \int_{-\ell_x+1}^{\infty} |\xi(t)|^2 dt$$

Consequently the expression (5.40) converges to $\|P_x\xi\|^2 + \|P_x\xi\|^2 - 2\|P_x\xi\|^2 = 0$ when $x' \to x$. This concludes the proof of the property (2) for $\{V_x\}_{x \geq 0}$. Q.E.D.

COROLLARY 5.5. (to Theorem 4.3). *The* C^**-algebra* $C^*(S_{PQ},\mathcal{G})$ *is isomorphic to*

$$(5.41)\quad A = \left\{ f \in C_0([0,\infty), M_2(\mathcal{K})) \;\middle|\; f(0) = \begin{pmatrix} f_1 & 0 \\ 0 & f_2 \end{pmatrix},\ f_1, f_2 \in \mathcal{K} \right\} .$$

COROLLARY 5.6. *An isomorphism* Φ_{PQ} *from* A'_{PQ} $(= C_0(S_{PQ}) \rtimes \mathbb{R})$ *onto* A $(= C^*(S_{PQ},\mathcal{G}))$ *is given by the following. For any continuous field of operators* $f' \in A'$ *(Lemma 5.2),* $f'(x) \in \mathcal{K}(P_x L^2(\mathbb{R}) \oplus Q_{-x} L^2(\mathbb{R}))$ *for* $t \in [0,\infty)$, *we let*

$$(5.42)\qquad f(x) = V_x f'(x) V_x^{-1} \in \mathcal{K}(L^2(\mathbb{R}) \oplus L^2(\mathbb{R}))$$

where $\{V_x\}$ *is given by Lemma 5.4.*

Proof. It is clear from Lemma 5.4 (2), that $x \longrightarrow f(x)$ is continuous in norm for $x \in [0,\infty)$. Moreover, that $f'(0) = \mathrm{diag}(f_1, f_2)$ implies that

$$f(0) = V_0 f'(0) V_0^{-1} = \begin{pmatrix} f_1 & 0 \\ 0 & f_2 \end{pmatrix}$$

has Property (1) of Lemma 5.4. It is easy to see that $\Phi_{PQ}: A'_{PQ} \longrightarrow A_{PQ}$ is a homomorphism which has an obvious inverse given by $f'(x) = V_x^{-1} f(x) V_x \in \mathcal{K}(P_x L^2(\mathbb{R}) \oplus Q_{-x} L^2(\mathbb{R}))$. Again by (1) and (2) we see (by triangle estimate) that $x \mapsto f(x)$ is continuous in norm iff $x \mapsto f'(x)$ is continuous in norm for $x \in [0,\infty)$ and also $f'(0) = f(0) = (f_1, f_2) \in \mathcal{K}^2$. Q.E.D.

Remark 5.7. Clearly all the C^*-algebra $C^*(S_{PQ},\mathcal{G})$ are the "same" for $P \in S^{p-1}$ and $Q \in S^{q-1}$, similarly for all the C^*-algebra $C_0(S_{PQ}) \rtimes \mathbb{R}$. We mentioned in §1 that the structure of the C^*-algebra $C^*(G(p,q))$ does not depend on the lengths $\alpha_1,\ldots,\alpha_{p+q}$ of the root vectors because this will not effect the quasi-equivalence class of the left Haar system. Thus we may assume that for every $P \in S^{p-1}$, $Q \in S^{q-1}$, we have fixed the same function ℓ_x on $(0,\infty)$ (see (5.1)).

Let A'_U be the C*-algebra of all the norm continuous functions

$$\begin{array}{l} f: S^{p-1} \times S^{q-1} \times [0,\infty) \longrightarrow \mathcal{K}(L^2(\mathbb{R}) \oplus L^2(\mathbb{R})) \quad \text{with} \\ \qquad\qquad\qquad\qquad\qquad\qquad\qquad \uparrow \text{inclusion} \\ (x,y,t) \longmapsto f(x,y,t) \in \mathcal{K}(P_tL^2(\mathbb{R}) \oplus Q_{-t}L^2(\mathbb{R})) \end{array}$$

such that f vanishes at infinity and

$$f(x,y,0) = \begin{pmatrix} f_1(x) & 0 \\ 0 & f_2(y) \end{pmatrix}, \qquad f_1(x), f_2(x) \in \mathcal{K}(L^2(\mathbb{R})) \quad . \tag{5.43}$$

In particular, $f_1 \in C(S^{p-1}, \mathcal{K}(L^2(\mathbb{R})))$, and $f_2 \in C(S^{q-1}, \mathcal{K}(L^2(\mathbb{R})))$.

COROLLARY 5.8. *There is a natural* C*-*algebra isomorphism from* $C_0(U) \rtimes \mathbb{R}$ *onto* A'_U.

<u>Proof</u>. In Lemma 5.2, for every $x \in S^{p-1}$, $y \in S^{q-1}$ we constructed a natural isomorphism $\hat{\psi}_{xy}$ which maps $C_0(S_{xy}) \rtimes_\sigma \mathbb{R}$ onto A'_{xy}, where S_{xy} is the quarter plane with boundary rays Ox and Oy.

For $g \in C_0(U) \rtimes \mathbb{R}$, we define $\hat{\psi}_1(g)(x,y) = \hat{\psi}_{xy}(g) \in A'$, where $A' = A'_{xy}$ for any $x \in S^{p-1}$ and $y \in S^{q-1}$. Let $\hat{\psi}_2$ be the obvious isomorphism from $C(S^{p-1} \times S^{q-1}, A')$ onto A'_U. Let $\hat{\psi} = \psi_2 \circ \psi_1$ which sends $C_0(U) \rtimes_\sigma \mathbb{R}$ to A'_U. We easily verify that

$$\hat{\psi}(g): (x,y,t) \mapsto (\hat{\psi}_{xy}g)(t) = \begin{pmatrix} P_t\pi_{N_t}^{(x,y)}(g)P_t & P_t\pi_{N_t}^{(x,y)}(g)Q_tU_t^* \\ U_tQ_t\pi_{N_t}^{(x,y)}(g)P_t & Q_{-t}\pi_{N_{-t}}^{(x,y)}(g)Q_{-t} \end{pmatrix} \in \tag{5.44}$$

$$\in \mathcal{K}(P_t L^2(\mathbb{R}) + Q_{-t} L^2(\mathbb{R}))$$

is norm continuous; see (5.9) and Figure 5.1.

If for some $g \in C^*(U, \mathcal{G})$, $\hat{\psi}(g) = 0$, then

$$(\hat{\psi}_{xy} g)(t) = 0 \quad \text{for all} \quad (x,y,t) \in S^{p-1} \times S^{q-1} \times (0,\infty) \quad .$$

By (5.31), for every $(x,y,t) \in S^{p-1} \times S^{q-1} \times (0,\infty)$, $\hat{\psi} g(x,y,t)$ is unitarily equivalent to $(\hat{\psi}_{xy} g)(t)$ for some $t > 0$. From Corollary 4.1 it follows that g=0. So $\hat{\psi}$ is an imbedding.

To verify that $\hat{\psi}$ is surjective, we show again the range of is a rich C^*-subalgebra of A_U'. This is rather easy, for different $(x,y,t) \in S^{p-1} \times S^{q-1} \times (0,\infty)$, the mapping

$$g \longmapsto \hat{\psi}_{xy} g(t)$$

gives mutual inequivalent irreducible representation of both $C^*(U,\mathcal{G})$ and A_U'. For every $(x,y,0) \in S^{p-1} \times S^{q-1} \times \{0\}$, we have two inequivalent irreducible representations of both $C^*(U,\mathcal{G})$ and A_U':

$$g \mapsto f_{1,g}(x) \qquad \text{and} \qquad g \mapsto f_{2,g}(y)$$

where

$$\begin{pmatrix} f_{1,g}(x) & 0 \\ 0 & f_{2,g}(y) \end{pmatrix} = \hat{\psi}_{xy} g(0) \quad .$$

That exhausts all irreducible representations of A_U' to unitary equivalence. Now we appeal to Dixmier's Proposition 11.16. Q.E.D.

Corresponding to Corollary 5.3, we have

PROPOSITION 5.9. *Assume the notation in Corollary 5.7. Let*

$A'_{U_1} = \{f \in A'_U \mid$ *corresponding to* $f_1(x) = f_2(y) = 0$ *for all* $x \in S^{p-1}$, $y \in S^{q-1}\}$

be an ideal of A'_U. *Recall the* A_X *given in Theorem 4.4. Then we have the following commuting diagram:*

$$(5.45)\qquad \begin{array}{ccccccccc} 0 & \longrightarrow & A'_U & \longrightarrow & A'_U & \xrightarrow{\pi'_X} & A_X & \longrightarrow & 0 \\ & & \Big\uparrow & & \Big\uparrow {\scriptstyle \simeq\,\hat{\psi}} & & \Big\uparrow {\scriptstyle \simeq} & & \\ 0 & \longrightarrow & C_0(U_1)\rtimes\mathbb{R} & \longrightarrow & C_0(U)\rtimes\mathbb{R} & \longrightarrow & C_0(X)\rtimes\mathbb{R} & \longrightarrow & 0 \end{array}$$

where $\pi'_X(f) = (f_1, f_2)$.

THEOREM 5.10. *Let* $A_{U_1} = C_0(S^{p-1} \times S^{q-1} \times (0,\infty),\, M_2(\mathcal{K}))$. *Then there is an isomorphism* Ψ *from* $C_0(U)\rtimes\mathbb{R}$ *onto* A_U *such that the following commutes:*

$$(5.46)\qquad \begin{array}{ccccccccc} 0 & \longrightarrow & A_{U_1} & \longrightarrow & A_U & \xrightarrow{\pi_X} & A_X & \longrightarrow & 0 \\ & & \Big\uparrow & & \Big\uparrow {\scriptstyle \simeq\,\Psi} & & \Big\uparrow {\scriptstyle \simeq} & & \\ 0 & \longrightarrow & C_0(U_1)\rtimes\mathbb{R} & \longrightarrow & C_0(U)\rtimes\mathbb{R} & \longrightarrow & C_0(X)\rtimes\mathbb{R} & \longrightarrow & 0 \end{array}$$

where $\pi_X(f) = (f_1, f_2)$.

Proof. We construct a natural isomorphism $\Phi\colon A'_U \to A_U$ by defining

$$(\Phi f')(x,y,t) \;=\; V_t f'(x,y,t) V'_t \;\in\; \mathcal{K}(L^2(\mathbb{R}) \oplus L^2(\mathbb{R}))$$

for any $f' \in A'$ and $(x,y,t) \in S^{p-1} \times S^{q-1} \times [0,\infty)$. It is straightforward to check that $\Phi f' \in A_U$ and that Φ is an isomorphism with the inverse given by

$(\Phi^{-1}f)(x,y,t) = V_t^{-1}f(x,y,t)V_t \in \mathcal{K}(P_tL^2(\mathbb{R}) \oplus Q_{-t}L^2(\mathbb{R}))$. Let $\Psi = \Phi \circ \hat{\psi}$. The rest of the assertions follow readily from Proposition 5.9. Q.E.D.

Now we have explicitly determine an isomorphism from $C_0(S_{PQ}) \rtimes \mathbb{R}$ onto $C^*(S_{PQ}, \mathcal{G})$. We shall continue the study of $C_0(\dot{S}_{PQ}) \rtimes \mathbb{R}$. Since $\pi_{N_+}(g)$ and $\pi_{N_-}(g)$ are not compact if $g \in C_0(\dot{S}_{PQ}) \rtimes \mathbb{R} \setminus C_0(S_{PQ}) \rtimes \mathbb{R}$ but the entries of $\hat{\psi}_{PQ}(g)$ are always compact, one cannot hope that the *-strong convergence in (5.12) can be replaced by convergence in norm. However, we'll be able to strengthen Lemma 5.1 in terms of norm convergence of a certain way. The idea is motivated by the observation that in the proof of Lemma 5.2, to estimate the expression (5.25) we had a rather strong condition ensuring $g(S\cdot N,t) = 0$ if $|S\cdot N| < \delta_0$ Actually if only the difference

$$|g(S\cdot N_x - t) - g(S\cdot N_+ - t)| = 0$$

in a neighborhood of 0, we are quite satisfied.

LEMMA 5.11. *Let*

$$\mathcal{D}_2 = \{f \in C_c(\mathbb{R}, C_c(\dot{S}_{PQ})) \mid \text{there is } \varepsilon_f > 0 \text{ such that for all } t, \ f(t) \text{ is constant in } B_0(\varepsilon_f) \cap \dot{S}_{PQ} \subset \mathbb{R}^2\} .$$

Then $\mathcal{D}_2$ *is a dense subalgebra of* $C_0(\dot{S}_{PQ}) \rtimes_\sigma \mathbb{R}$.

<u>Proof</u>. We have to show that indeed $\mathcal{D}_2$ is a subalgebra. Let $f,g \in \mathcal{D}_2$. Then

$$f * g_t = \int_{s\in\mathbb{R}} f_s\sigma_s(g_{t-s})ds \in C_c(\dot{S}_{PQ}), \qquad t \in \mathbb{R}$$

(5.47)

$$f * g_t(x,y) = \int_{\mathbb{R}} f_s(x,y)g_{t-s}(\sigma_{-s}(x,y))ds .$$

There is $N_0 > 0$ such that $f_t=0$, $g_t=0$ for $|t| > N_0$. Because 0 is a fixed point of σ, and the $\mathbb{R}$-action σ is continuous, so there exists $\varepsilon_{f*g} > 0$ such that when $|(x,y)| < \varepsilon_{f*g}$ then $|\sigma_s(x,y)| < \min\{\varepsilon_f, \varepsilon_g\}$ for all $|s| < N_0$.

It follows from (5.47) that $f*g_t$ is constant inside $\{|(x,y)| < \varepsilon_{f*g}\}$ for all $t \in \mathbb{R}$.

It is straightforward to verify that $\mathcal{D}_2$ is dense in $C_c(\mathbb{R}, C_c(\dot{S}_{PQ}))$, thus in $C_0(\dot{S}_{PQ}) \rtimes \mathbb{R}$. We omit the routine estimate. Q.E.D.

LEMMA 5.12. *Assume the notation in Lemmas 5.1 and 5.2. For any* $g \in C(\dot{S}_{PQ}) \rtimes_\sigma \mathbb{R}$, *we have the following when* $x \to 0$ *(cf.* (5.2)*)*:

(5.48) $$P_x(\pi_{N_x}(g) - \pi_{N_+}(g)) \xrightarrow{\text{norm}} 0$$

(5.49) $$Q_{-x}(\pi_{N_{-x}}(g) - \pi_{N_-}(g)) \xrightarrow{\text{norm}} 0$$

(5.50) $$Q_x(\pi_{N_x}(g) - \pi_{N_+}(g))P_x \xrightarrow{\text{norm}} 0$$

(5.51) $$P_{-x}(\pi_{N_{-x}}(g) - \pi_{N_-}(g))Q_{-x} \xrightarrow{\text{norm}} 0 \quad .$$

Proof. We prove only (5.48) and (5.50). Then (5.49) and (5.51) will follow from symmetry. By Lemma 5.11, we may assume that $g \in \mathcal{D}_2$, so that there are constants $N > \varepsilon_g > 0$ such that

1) $\operatorname{supp}(g) \subset B_0(N)$

2) For each $t \in \mathbb{R}$, $g_t(P) = g(P,t)$ is constant on $\{|P| < \varepsilon_g\}$.

A straightforward computation shows (see (5.25)),

$$(5.52)\qquad \|P_x(\pi_{N_x}(g) - \pi_{N_+}(g)\| \le \int_{-\ell_x}^{\infty}\int_{-\infty}^{\infty} |g(s\cdot N_x,t) - g(s\cdot N_+,t)|^2\, dtds$$

$$= \int_{-\ell_x}^{\infty}\int_{-N}^{N} |g(s\cdot N_x,t) - g(s\cdot N_+,t)|^2\, dtds\ .$$

Again there are some $L_N > 0$ and $L_{\varepsilon_g} > 0$ such that when $s > L_N$ then $|s\cdot N_x| > N$, $|s\cdot N_+| > N$ for $0 < x < \varepsilon_g/2$, and that when $-\ell_x < s < -L_{\varepsilon_g}$ then

$$|s\cdot N_x| < \varepsilon_g \qquad \text{and} \qquad |s\cdot N_+| < \varepsilon_g$$

for all $0 < x < \varepsilon_g/2$.

Therefore if $0 < x < \varepsilon_g/2$ then the expression (5.52) becomes

$$(5.53)\qquad \int_{-L_{\varepsilon_g}}^{L_N}\int_{-N}^{N} |g(s\cdot N_x,t) - g(s\cdot N_+,t)|^2\, dtds \quad .$$

Now by the continuity of g we see that the expressions (5.25') and (5.53) converge to 0 as $x \to 0$ (see the discussion after (5.25')). Thus (5.48) is true. Taking adjoints in (5.48), we have

$$(5.54)\qquad (\pi_{N_x}(g) - \pi_{N_+}(g))P_x \xrightarrow{\text{norm}} 0$$

for any $g \in C(\dot{S}_{PQ}) \rtimes_\sigma \mathbb{R}$. Now (5.50) follows from (5.54). Q.E.D.

We'll use the following elementary fact later.

<u>Remark 5.13</u>. For $g \in C_0(\dot{S}_{PQ}) \rtimes_\sigma \mathbb{R} \setminus C_0(S_{PQ}) \rtimes_\sigma \mathbb{R}$, the following is *false*:

$$Q_x(\pi_{N_x}(g) - \pi_{N_+}(g))Q_x \xrightarrow{\text{norm}} 0$$

or

$$P_{-x}(\pi_{N_{-x}}(g) - \pi_{N_-}(g))P_{-x} \xrightarrow{\text{norm}} 0 \qquad \text{as} \quad x \to 0\ .$$

Equivalently (compare (5.50), (5.51)),

$$Q_x(\pi_{N_x}(g) - \pi_{N_+}(g)) \xrightarrow{\text{norm}} 0$$

and

$$P_{-x}(\pi_{N_{-x}}(g) - \pi_{N_-}(g)) \xrightarrow{\text{norm}} 0 \quad \text{as} \quad x \to 0$$

are *false.*

LEMMA 5.14. *Suppose that there is an exact sequence of* C^**-algebras*

$$0 \longrightarrow I \longrightarrow E \longrightarrow C(S^1) \longrightarrow 0 \quad .$$

Let $T \in p^{-1}(z)$. *Here* z *is the identity function on* S^1. *Then*

$$\mathcal{D} = \{a + \sum_{\text{finite}} a_{ij} \, T^i T^{*j} \mid a \in I,\ a_{ij} \in \mathbb{C}\} \tag{5.55}$$

is a dense subalgebra of E.

<u>Proof</u>. It is clear that $\mathcal{D}$ is a subalgebra of E and that $p(\mathcal{D})$ is dense in $C(S^1)$. Take any $b \in E$, there exists some $f = p(d) \in p(\mathcal{D})$ such that $\|p(b) - f\| \leq \varepsilon$ for a given $\varepsilon > 0$. Since

$$\|p(b) - f\| = \|p(b-d)\| = \inf_{a \in I} \|b - d + a\| \quad ,$$

thus $\|b - d + a\| \leq 2\varepsilon$ for some $a \in I$. Q.E.D.

LEMMA 5.15. *Assume the notations introduced in the beginning of this section. For any* $g \in C(\dot{S}_{PQ}) \rtimes \mathbb{R}$, *we define* $\hat{\psi}'_{PQ}g(x)$, $\hat{\psi}''_{PQ}g(x)$ *by*

$$\hat{\psi}'_{PQ}g(x) = \begin{pmatrix} P_x \pi_{N_+}(g) P_x & P_x \pi_{N_+}(g) Q_x U_x^* \\ U_x Q_x \pi_{N_+}(g) P_x & Q_{-x} \pi_{N_-}(g) Q_{-x} \end{pmatrix} \tag{5.56}$$

and

$$(5.57) \qquad \hat{\psi}''_{PQ}g(x) = \begin{pmatrix} \sim & U_x^* P_{-x}\pi_{N_-}(g)Q_{-x} \\ \sim & \sim \end{pmatrix} .$$

Then $\hat{\psi}'_{PQ}g(x)$, $\hat{\psi}''_{PQ}g(x) \in \mathcal{K}(P_xL^2(\mathbb{R}) \oplus Q_{-x}L^2(\mathbb{R}))$ *and*

$$(5.58) \qquad \hat{\psi}_{PQ}g(x) - \hat{\psi}'_{PQ}g(x) \xrightarrow{\text{norm}} 0$$

$$(5.59) \qquad \hat{\psi}_{PQ}g(x) - \hat{\psi}''_{PQ}g(x) \xrightarrow{\text{norm}} 0$$

when $x \to 0$.

Proof. It is clear that $\hat{\psi}'_{PQ}g(x)$, $\hat{\psi}''_{PQ}g(x) \in \mathcal{B}(P_xL^2(\mathbb{R}) \oplus Q_{-x}L^2(\mathbb{R}))$. We claim that both $P_x\pi_{N_+}(g)$ and $Q_{-x}\pi_{N_-}(g)$ are compact. From (5.56) and (5.57) it then follows that $\psi'_{PQ}g(x)$ and $\psi''_{PQ}g(x)$ are also compact.

By Lemma 5.13, the subalgebra

$$\mathcal{D}_1^+ = \{a + \sum a_{ij}(1+\hat{\psi}_{PQ}g_0)^n(1+\hat{\psi}_{PQ}g_0)^{*m} \mid a \in C_0(S_{PQ}) \rtimes_\sigma \mathbb{R}\}$$

is dense in $(C_0(\dot{S}_{PQ}) \rtimes_\sigma \mathbb{R})^+$, and that the subalgebra

$$(5.60) \qquad \mathcal{D}_1 = \{a + \sum a_{ij}(\hat{\psi}_{PQ}g_0)^n(\hat{\psi}_{PQ}g_0)^{*m} \mid a \in C_0(S_{PQ}) \rtimes_\sigma \mathbb{R}\}$$

is dense in $C_0(\dot{S}_{PQ}) \rtimes_\sigma \mathbb{R}$, where g_0 is defined by (2.25).

By Lemma 5.2, $\pi_{N_+}(a)$ is compact for $a \in C_0(S_{PQ}) \rtimes_\sigma \mathbb{R}$. So it suffices to show that $P_x\pi_{N_+}(g_0)$ is compact for $x > 0$. By definition

$$(5.61) \qquad P_x\pi_{N_+}(g_0)\xi(s) = -\chi_{[\frac{1}{2}\ln x,\infty)}(s)\,\hat{h}(0,e^s)\int_0^\infty e^{-t/2}\,\xi(s-t)dt .$$

Thus $P_x\pi_{N_+}(g_0)$ is obviously a Hilbert-Schmidt operator (see Figure 5.4) so it is compact.

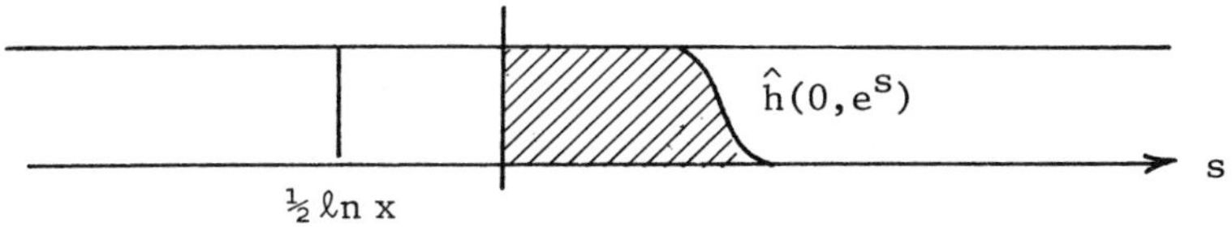

Figure 5.4

By "symmetry", $Q_{-x}\pi_{N_-}(g_0)$ is also compact. Since

$$\hat{\psi}_{PQ}g(x) - \hat{\psi}'_{PQ}g(x) = \begin{pmatrix} P_x(\pi_{N_x}(g) - \pi_{N_+}(g))P_x & P_x(\pi_{N_x}(g) - \pi_{N_+}(g))Q_xU_x^* \\ U_xQ_x(\pi_{N_x}(g) - \pi_{N_+}(g))P_x & Q_{-x}(\pi_{N_{-x}}(g) - \pi_{N_-}(g))Q_{-x} \end{pmatrix}$$

Lemma 5.12 implies (5.58).

Analogously for (5.59). We note that (see (5.3))

$$U_x^*P_{-x}\pi_{N_{-x}}(g)Q_{-x} = P_x\pi_{N_x}(g)Q_xU_x^* \quad .$$ Q.E.D.

Note that the mapping $g \mapsto \hat{\psi}'_{PQ}g(x)$ is *not* a representation of $C_c(\dot{S}_{PQ}) \rtimes_\sigma \mathbb{R}$. The same warning applies to $\hat{\psi}''_{PQ}$. Notice also that (5.56)-(5.59) imply that

$$P_x\pi_{N_+}(g)Q_xU_x^* - U_x^*P_{-x}\pi_{N_-}(g)Q_{-x} \xrightarrow{\text{norm}} 0$$

as $x \to 0$. Put differently,

$$P_x\pi_{N_+}(g)Q_xU_x^* - P_x(U_x^*\pi_{N_-}(g)U_x)Q_xU_x^* \xrightarrow{\text{norm}} 0$$

i.e.

(5.62) $$P_x(\pi_{N_+}(g) - U_x^*\pi_{N_-}(g)U_x)Q_x \xrightarrow{\text{norm}} 0 \quad .$$

Since both $\pi_{N_+}(g)$ and $\pi_{N_-}(g)$ can be noncompact and selected only by a single relation: $\pi(\pi_{N_+}(g)) = \overline{\pi(\pi_{N_-}(g))}$, that (5.62) is by no means obvious.

LEMMA 5.16. *Assume the notation of Lemmas 5.1 and 5.15. Extend the definition of* $\hat{\psi}'_{PQ}$ *and* $\hat{\psi}''_{PQ}$ *to* $\bar{A}'$ *by replacing* $(\pi_{N_+}(g), \pi_{N_-}(g))$ *with* (f_1,f_2) *in* (5.56) *and* (5.57). *In addition let*

$$\hat{\psi}'_{PQ}f(0) = \hat{\psi}''_{PQ}f(0) = f(0) = \begin{pmatrix} f_1 & 0 \\ 0 & f_2 \end{pmatrix}. \tag{5.62}$$

Then $\hat{\psi}'_{PQ}$ *and* $\hat{\psi}''_{PQ}$ *are linear mappings from* $\bar{A}'$ *into* $C(\dot{S}_{PQ}) \rtimes_\sigma \mathbb{R} \subset \bar{A}'$.

Proof. Consider the exact sequence (see (2.9))

(5.63)
$$0 \longrightarrow C_0(\mathring{S}_{PQ}) \rtimes_\sigma \mathbb{R} \longrightarrow C_0(\dot{S}_{PQ}) \rtimes_\sigma \mathbb{R} \xrightarrow{\pi_X|\dot{S}_{PQ}} C_0(OP \vee OQ) \rtimes_\sigma \mathbb{R} \longrightarrow 0$$

Given any $f \in \bar{A}'$ then $f(0) = (f_1,f_2) \in C_0(OP \vee OQ) \rtimes_\sigma \mathbb{R}$. So there is some $g \in \pi_X|_{\dot{S}_{PQ}}^{-1}(f(0)) \subset C_0(\dot{S}_{PQ}) \rtimes_\sigma \mathbb{R}$ with $(f_1,f_2) = (\pi_{N_+}(g), \pi_{N_-}(g))$. Thus $\hat{\psi}'_{PQ}f = \hat{\psi}'_{PQ}g$ and $\hat{\psi}''_{PQ}f = \hat{\psi}''_{PQ}g$.

We need to show first that the mappings

$$x \longmapsto \hat{\psi}'_{PQ}g(x) \quad , \qquad x \longmapsto \hat{\psi}''_{PQ}g(x)$$

are norm continuous for $x > 0$. If we can show that for $x \in (0,\infty)$

$$x \longmapsto P_x\pi_{N_+}(g) \tag{5.64}$$

is norm continuous, then symmetrically the mapping

$$x \longmapsto Q_{-x}\pi_{N_-}(g)$$

is also norm continuous. Since both $P_x\pi_{N_+}(g)$ and $Q_{-x}\pi_{N_-}(g)$ are compact for $x > 0$ by Lemma 6.4 and the mappings $x \mapsto P_x$, $x \mapsto Q_x$, $x \mapsto U_x$ are *-strong continuous, it follows that for $x \in (0,\infty)$, the mappings

$$x \to P_x \pi_{N_+}(g) P_x \quad , \qquad x \to P_x \pi_{N_+}(g) Q_x U_x^*$$

$$x \to Q_{-x} \pi_{N_-}(g) Q_{-x} \quad , \qquad x \to U_x^* P_{-x} \pi_{N_-}(g) Q_{-x}$$

are all norm continuous. So are the mappings

$$x \to \hat{\psi}'_{PQ} g(x) \qquad \text{and} \qquad x \to \hat{\psi}''_{PQ} g(x) \quad .$$

So it boils down to checking (5.64).

Let $0 < x \leq x'$. We want

$$\| P_x \pi_{N_+}(g) - P_{x'} \pi_{N_+}(g) \| \to 0 \quad \text{as} \quad x' \searrow x \quad . \tag{5.65}$$

Since $P_{x'} \leq P_x$ and $P_x \pi_{N_+}(g)$ are compact, so

$$\begin{aligned} \| P_x \pi_{N_+}(g) - P_{x'} \pi_{N_+}(g) \| &= \| P_x \pi_{N_+}(g) - P_{x'} P_x \pi_{N_+}(g) \| \\ &= \| (P_x - P_{x'}) P_x \pi_{N_+}(g) \| \to 0 \end{aligned}$$

as $x' \searrow x$. Thus $\hat{\psi}'_{PQ} f$ and $\hat{\psi}''_{PQ} f$ are in $\bar{A}'$ for any $f \in \bar{A}'$. Since $\hat{\psi}'_{PQ} g(x) - g(x) \xrightarrow{\text{norm}} 0$ as $x \to 0$ by Lemma 6.4, so $(\hat{\psi}'_{PQ} g - g) \in C_0(\mathring{S}_{PQ}) \rtimes_\sigma \mathbb{R}$. Hence

$$\hat{\psi}'_{PQ} f = \hat{\psi}'_{PQ} g = g + (\hat{\psi}'_{PQ} g - g) \in C_0(\mathring{S}_{PQ}) \rtimes_\sigma \mathbb{R} \quad .$$

The same is true for $\hat{\psi}''_{PQ} f$. Q.E.D.

Summarizing the preceding, we have a nice criterion which characterizes $C_0(\mathring{S}_{PQ}) \rtimes_\sigma \mathbb{R}$ as a (separable) C^*-subalgebra of $\bar{A}'$:

LEMMA 5.17. *Assume the notation in Lemmas 5.1 and 5.15. For any* $f \in \bar{A}'$, f *is contained in the* C^**-subalgebra* $C_0(\dot{S}_{PQ}) \rtimes_\sigma \mathbb{R}$ *of* $\bar{A}'$ *if and only if* $\hat{\psi}'_{PQ}f(x) - f(x) \to 0$ *in norm when* $x \to 0$, *i.e.* $\hat{\psi}'_{PQ}f - f \in C_0(\mathring{S}_{PQ}) \rtimes_\sigma \mathbb{R}$. *The same is true for* $\hat{\psi}''_{PQ}$.

Proof. "Only if" is given by Lemma 5.15. To see the sufficiency, using Lemma 5.16, we have $\hat{\psi}'_{PQ}f \in C_0(\dot{S}_{PQ}) \rtimes_\sigma \mathbb{R}$, so

$$f = f + (\hat{\psi}'_{PQ}f - f) \in C_0(\dot{S}_{PQ}) \rtimes_\sigma \mathbb{R} \quad . \qquad \text{Q.E.D.}$$

Remark 5.18. Although we have (5.14), we do not expect that

$$\|\pi_{N_x}(g)\| \longrightarrow \|\pi_{N_+}(g)\|, \qquad x \to 0$$

and

$$\|\pi_{N_{-x}}(g)\| \longrightarrow \|\pi_{N_-}(g)\|, \qquad x \to 0$$

even for g in the ideal $C_0(S_{PQ}) \rtimes_\sigma \mathbb{R}$ of $C_0(\dot{S}_{PQ}) \rtimes_\sigma \mathbb{R}$. In fact, $\pi_{N_x}(g)$ is unitarily equivalent to $\pi_{N_{-x}}(g)$ so that $\|\pi_{N_x}(g)\| = \|\pi_{N_{-x}}(g)\|$, but $\|\pi_{N_+}(g)\|$ and $\|\pi_{N_-}(g)\|$ can differ by anything in the world.

Now we can shed some light on this mystery and it has become an easy routine.

LEMMA 5.18. *Assume the notation in Lemma 5.1. Then in addition to* (5.12) *we have*

$$\|P_x\pi_{N_x}(g)P_x\| \longrightarrow \|\pi_{N_+}(g)\| \tag{5.66}$$

$$\|Q_{-x}\pi_{N_{-x}}(g)P_{-x}\| \longrightarrow \|\pi_{N_-}(g)\| \tag{5.67}$$

and (see (5.9)*),*

$$(5.68) \qquad \|\hat{\psi}_{PQ}g(x)\| \longrightarrow \left\| \begin{pmatrix} \pi_{N_+}(g) & 0 \\ 0 & \pi_{N_-}(g) \end{pmatrix} \right\|$$

$$= \max(\|\pi_{N_+}(g)\|, \ \|\pi_{N_-}(g)\|)$$

for any $g \in C_0(\dot{S}_{PQ}) \rtimes_\alpha \mathbb{R}$.

Remark 5.19. As a consequence we have

$$(5.69) \qquad \|\pi_{0_x}(g)\| = \|\pi_{N_x}(g)\| = \|\pi_{N_{-x}}(g)\| \longrightarrow \max(\|\pi_{N_+}(g)\|, \|\pi_{N_-}(g)\|)$$

see (5.22) and (5.5). Note that

$$\|P_x \pi_{N_x}(g) Q_x U_x^*\| \longrightarrow 0$$

is still *false* in general for $g \in C_0(\dot{S}_{PQ}) \rtimes_\sigma \mathbb{R}$. Compare (5.28).

Proof of Lemma 5.18. From (5.48) we have

$$\left| \|P_x \pi_{N_x}(g) P_x\| - \|P_x \pi_{N_+}(g) P_x\| \right| \longrightarrow 0 \quad \text{as} \quad x \to 0 .$$

Thus to see (5.66), it suffices to show

$$(5.70) \qquad \|P_x \pi_{N_+}(g) P_x\| \longrightarrow \|\pi_{N_+}(g)\| .$$

On one hand we have

$$(5.71) \qquad \|P_x \pi_{N_+}(g) P_x\| \leq \|\pi_{N_+}(g)\| .$$

On the other, by Lemma 5.1, we have

$$P_x \pi_{N_+}(g) P_x \xrightarrow{*-st} \pi_{N_+}(g) , \qquad x \to 0$$

so that

$$\text{(5.72)} \qquad \liminf_{x\to 0} \|P_x \pi_{N_+}(g) P_x\| \geq \|\pi_{N_+}(g)\| \quad .$$

Combine (5.71) and (5.72), we get (5.70) as well as (5.66).

Similarly (5.67) holds.

By Lemma 5.15, to show (5.68) it is equivalent to show that

$$\text{(5.73)} \qquad \hat{\psi}'_{PQ} g(x) = \begin{pmatrix} P_x \pi_{N_x}(g) P_x & P_x \pi_{N_+}(g) Q_x U_x^* \\ U_x Q_x \pi_{N_+}(g) P_x & Q_{-x} \pi_{N_-}(g) Q_{-x} \end{pmatrix}$$

$$\longrightarrow \max(\|\pi_{N_+}(g)\| , \|\pi_{N_-}(g)\|) \qquad \text{as} \quad x \to 0 \quad .$$

It is obvious that

$$\|\hat{\psi}'_{PQ} g(x)\| \leq \max(\|\pi_{N_+}(g)\| , \|\pi_{N_-}(g)\|) \quad .$$

In the other direction we notice that

$$\hat{\psi}'_{PQ} g(x) \xrightarrow{*\text{-st}} \begin{pmatrix} \pi_{N_+}(g) & 0 \\ 0 & \pi_{N_-}(g) \end{pmatrix} \qquad \text{as} \quad x \to 0$$

so that again

$$\liminf_{x\to 0} \|\hat{\psi}'_{PQ} g(x)\| \geq \left\| \begin{pmatrix} \pi_{N_+}(g) & 0 \\ 0 & \pi_{N_-}(g) \end{pmatrix} \right\|$$

Thus (5.73) holds and so does (5.68). Q.E.D.

Let $\bar{C}'$ be the (nonseparable) C^*-algebra of all norm continuous bounded functions

$$\begin{array}{rcl} f\colon (0,\infty) & \longrightarrow & \mathcal{K}(L^2(\mathbb{R}) \oplus L^2(\mathbb{R})) \\ & & \quad \uparrow \\ t & \longmapsto & f(t) \in \mathcal{K}(P_x L^2(\mathbb{R}) \oplus Q_{-x} L^2(\mathbb{R})) \end{array}$$

Our first description for $C_0(\dot{S}_{PQ}) \rtimes_\sigma \mathbb{R}$ is (compare with Corollary 5.5)

THEOREM 5.20. *The natural imbedding* $\hat{\psi}_{PQ}$ *identifies* $C_0(\dot{S}_{PQ}) \rtimes_\sigma \mathbb{R}$ *with a C*-subalgebra of* $\bar{C}'$ *such that for any* $f \in C_0(\dot{S}_{PQ}) \rtimes_\sigma \mathbb{R}$, *we have*

i) $f(x) \xrightarrow{\text{norm}} 0$ *as* x

ii) $f(x) \xrightarrow{*\text{-st}} \begin{pmatrix} f_1 & 0 \\ 0 & f_2 \end{pmatrix}$, *as* $x \to 0$ *where*

$(f_1, f_2) \in C^*((S^*-I) \oplus 0) \oplus C^*(0 \oplus (S-I))$, $\pi(f_1) = \overline{\pi(f_2)}$.

iii) $\|f(x)\| \longrightarrow \left\| \begin{pmatrix} f_1 & 0 \\ 0 & f_2 \end{pmatrix} \right\|$ *as* $x \to 0$.

We have the following exact sequences:

$$\begin{array}{ccccccccc} 0 & \longrightarrow & C_0(\mathring{S}_{PQ}) \rtimes \mathbb{R} & \longrightarrow & C_0(\dot{S}_{PQ}) \rtimes \mathbb{R} & \longrightarrow & C_0(OP \vee OQ) \rtimes_\sigma \mathbb{R} & \longrightarrow & 0 \\ & & \| & & \| & & \| & & \\ 0 & \longrightarrow & \{f \in \bar{C}' \mid f(t) \xrightarrow[t \to 0]{\text{norm}} 0\} & \longrightarrow & C_0(\dot{S}_{PQ}) \rtimes \mathbb{R} & \longrightarrow & \{(f_1,f_2) \in C^*((S^*-I) \oplus 0) \oplus C^*(0 \oplus (S-I))\} \text{ s.t. } \pi(f_1) = \overline{\pi(f_2)} & \longrightarrow & 0 \\ & & & & f & \longrightarrow & (f_1, f_2) & & \end{array}$$

(5.74)

Proof. It follows from Lemmas 5.1 and 5.18. Q.E.D.

Remark 5.21. Although $\bar{C}'$ is huge, any C*-subalgebra E of $\bar{C}'$ which satisfies (i), (ii) and (iii) is separable. In fact for every $(f_1, f_2) \in C_0(OP \vee OQ) \rtimes_\sigma \mathbb{R}$, fix an element $f_{(f_1,f_2)} \in E$ such that (ii) holds. Now let $f \in E$, such that $f(x) \xrightarrow[*\text{-st}]{} \begin{pmatrix} f_1 & 0 \\ 0 & f_2 \end{pmatrix}$ when $x \to 0$ for the same (f_1, f_2). Since $f - f_{(f_1,f_2)} \in E$, (iii) forces $f - f_{(f_1,f_2)}$ $C_0(\mathring{S}_{PQ}) \rtimes \mathbb{R}$. Thus E is an extension of $C_0(\mathring{S}_{PQ}) \rtimes \mathbb{R}$ by $C_0(OP \vee OQ) \rtimes \mathbb{R}$ and is separable in particular.

It follows trivially that such a C*-subalgebra E is "unique" or "maximal" in the sense that E is not contained in (or does not contain) any other C*-subalgebra E' of $\bar{C}'$ which satisfies (i), (ii) and (iii).

The description given by Theorem 5.20 does not pinpoint $C_0(\dot{S}_{PQ}) \rtimes \mathbb{R}$ as a subalgebra of $\bar{C}'$ which satisfies condition (i), (ii) and (iii). We note that the fact that $f, f' \in \bar{C}'$ satisfies (i), (ii) and (ii) does not imply $f + f'$ satisfies (iii).

We have a second description for $C_0(S_{PQ}) \rtimes_\sigma \mathbb{R}$.

THEOREM 5.21 *The natural imbedding* $\hat{\psi}_{PQ}$ *identifies* $C_0(\dot{S}_{PQ}) \rtimes_\sigma \mathbb{R}$ *with the* C*-*subalgebra of* $\bar{C}'$ *generated by the ideal* A' *(see Lemma 5.2) and one more generator*

$$(5.75) \qquad \hat{\psi}'_{PQ} g : x \longmapsto \begin{pmatrix} P_x((S^*-I)\oplus 0)P_x & P_x((S^*-I)\oplus 0)Q_x U_x^* \\ U_x Q_x((S^*-I)\oplus 0)P_x & Q_{-x}(0\oplus(S-I))Q_{-x} \end{pmatrix}.$$

(see (5.56)). The following sequence is exact:

$$(5.76) \qquad \begin{array}{ccccccccc} 0 & \longrightarrow & C_0(S_{PQ}) \rtimes_\sigma \mathbb{R} & \longrightarrow & C_0(\dot{S}_{PQ}) \rtimes_\sigma \mathbb{R} & \longrightarrow & C_0(\mathbb{R}) & \longrightarrow & 0 \\ & & \| & & \| & & \| & & \\ 0 & \longrightarrow & A' & \longrightarrow & C_0(\dot{S}_{PQ}) \rtimes_\sigma \mathbb{R} & \xrightarrow{\pi_0} & C_0(\mathbb{R}) & \longrightarrow & 0 \\ & & & & \hat{\psi}'_{PQ} g_0 & \longmapsto & \theta - 1 & & \end{array}$$

(see (2.26)). So a dense subalgebra of $C_0(\dot{S}_{PQ}) \rtimes_\sigma \mathbb{R}$ *is given by Lemma 5.12 with* $A' = I$ *and* $T = \hat{\psi}'_{PQ} g$.

<u>Proof</u>. By Lemma 5.2 we have $C_0(S_{PQ}) \rtimes_\sigma \mathbb{R} \cong A'$ is an ideal of $C_0(\dot{S}_{PQ}) \rtimes_\sigma \mathbb{R}$. From Theorem 2.5 we have

$$(5.77)\qquad 0 \longrightarrow C^*(\mathcal{L},\mathcal{Q}) \longrightarrow C_0(OP \vee OQ) \rtimes_\sigma \mathbb{R} \longrightarrow C_0(\mathbb{R}) \longrightarrow 0$$
$$\pi_x|_{\dot{S}_{PQ}} \cdot \hat{\psi}_{PQ} g_0 \longmapsto \theta - 1$$

(see (5.63) and (2.11). Lemma 5.16 implies that $\hat{\psi}'_{PQ} g_0 \in C_0(\dot{S}_{PQ}) \rtimes_\sigma \mathbb{R}$ and $\pi'_0(\hat{\psi}'_{PQ} g\ ) = \pi'_0(\hat{\psi}_{PQ} g_0) = -1$. Now apply (5.74). Q.E.D.

Lemma 5.17 gives us the following third description of $C_0(\dot{S}_{PQ}) \rtimes_\sigma \mathbb{R}$. In a way it is more satisfactory.

THEOREM 5.22. *The* C^**-subalgebra* $C_0(\dot{S}_{PQ}) \rtimes_\sigma \mathbb{R}$ *of* $\bar{C}'$ *is characterized by*

$$(5.78)\qquad C_0(\dot{S}_{PQ}) \rtimes \mathbb{R} = \{f \in \bar{A}' \mid (\hat{\psi}'_{PQ} f)(x) - f(x) \xrightarrow{\text{norm}} 0 \text{ as } x \to 0\}$$

where $\bar{A}' \subset \bar{C}'$ *is defined in Lemma 5.1 and the mapping* $\hat{\psi}'_{PQ}$ *is defined in Lemma 5.15 (see (5.56)). The same is true for* $\hat{\psi}''_{PQ}$ *(see (5.57)).*

A shortcoming of Theorems 5.20 - 5.22 is that the fiber Hilbert spaces and the fiber C^*-algebras are not constant. This can be overcome by applying Lemma 5.4. We see that the continuous field of Hilbert spaces can be made globally trivial by means of a family of isometries $\{V_x\}, \{V_x^{-1}\}$. We even constructed $\{V_x\}, \{V_x^{-1}\}$ explicitly, see (5.34)-(5.38).

Recall from (5.42) that $\{Ad_{V_x}\}$ given correspondingly by the spatial isomorphism from $\mathcal{K}(P_x L^2(\mathbb{R}) \oplus Q_{-x} L^2(\mathbb{R}))$ to $\mathcal{K}(L^2(\mathbb{R}) \oplus L^2(\mathbb{R}))$:

$$(5.42')\qquad f(x) \longmapsto Ad_{V_x}(f'(x)) = V_x f'(x) V_x^{-1}$$

$$\begin{array}{ccc} P_xL^2(\mathbb{R}) \oplus Q_{-x}L^2(\mathbb{R}) & \xrightarrow{V_x} & L^2(\mathbb{R}) \oplus L^2(\mathbb{R}) \\ \downarrow f'(x) & & \downarrow f(x) = Ad_{V_x}(f'(x)) \\ P_xL^2(\mathbb{R}) \oplus Q_{-x}L^2(\mathbb{R}) & \xrightarrow[V_x^-]{} & L^2(\mathbb{R}) \oplus L^2(\mathbb{R}) \end{array}$$

Recall also that $V_x = (V^+, V^-)$, $V_x^{-1} = (V_x^{+-1}, V_x^{--1})$ both strongly converge to I when $x \to 0$ and that

(5.79) $\quad x \longmapsto f'(x)$ continuous in norm

$$\Longleftrightarrow x \longmapsto f(x) = Ad_{V_x}(f'(x)) \text{ continuous in norm .}$$

Because $\{V_x\}$, $\{V_x^{-1}\}$ are bounded, so $f(x) \xrightarrow{*\text{-st}} f(0) \Longleftrightarrow f'(x) \xrightarrow{*\text{-st}} f'(0)$ when $x \to 0$. Note $f(0) = f'(0)$.

Now it is easily seen that the preceding Theorems 5.20, 5.21 and 5.22 are equivalent to the following.

THEOREM 5.20'. *The natural imbedding* $\Psi_{PQ} = Ad_V \circ \hat{\psi}_{PQ}$ *identifies* $C_0(\dot{S}_{PQ}) \rtimes_\sigma \mathbb{R}$ *with a* C^**-subalgebra of*

(5.80) $\quad \bar{C} = C^b((0,\infty), M_2(\mathcal{K}(L^2(\mathbb{R}))))$

containing $C_0((0,\infty), M_2(\mathcal{K}(L^2(\mathbb{R}))))$ *such that for any* $f \in C_0(\dot{S}_{PQ}) \rtimes_\sigma \mathbb{R}$ *we have*

i) $f(x) \xrightarrow{\text{norm}} 0$ *as* $x \to \infty$.

ii) $f(x) \xrightarrow{*\text{-st}} \begin{pmatrix} f_1 & 0 \\ 0 & f_2 \end{pmatrix}$ *as* $x \to 0$ *where*

$(f_1, f_2) \in C^*(S^*-I) \oplus 0) \oplus C^*(0 \oplus (S-I))$, $\pi(f_1) = \overline{\pi(f_2)}$.

iii) $\|f(x)\| \longrightarrow \left\| \begin{pmatrix} f_1 & 0 \\ 0 & f_2 \end{pmatrix} \right\|$ *as* $x \to 0$.

And we have exact sequences (6.40) *with* $\bar{C}'$ *replaced by* $\bar{C}$.

THEOREM 5.21'. *The natural imbedding* Ψ_{PQ} *identifies* $C_0(\dot{S}_{PQ}) \rtimes_\sigma \mathbb{R}$ *with the* C^**-subalgebra of* $\bar{C}$ *generated by the ideal* A *(see Theorem 5.3) with one more generator:*

$$x \longmapsto V_x \hat{\psi}'_{PQ} g_0(x) V_x^{-1} \quad .$$

see (5.75).

THEOREM 5.22'. *Let* $\bar{A}$ *be the (non-separable)* C^**-algebra*

$\bar{A} = \Big\{ f \in C^b((0,\infty), M_2(\mathcal{K}(L^2(\mathbb{R})))$ *such that*

i) $f(x) \xrightarrow{\text{norm}} 0, \quad x \to \infty$.

ii) $f(x) \xrightarrow{*\text{-st}} \begin{pmatrix} f_1 & 0 \\ 0 & f_2 \end{pmatrix}$ *as* $x \to 0$ *where*

$(f_1, f_2) \in C^*((S^*-I) \oplus 0) \oplus C^*(0 \oplus (S-i)), \quad \pi(f_1) = \overline{\pi(f_2)} \Big\}$.

Then $C_0(\dot{S}_{PQ}) \rtimes \mathbb{R} = \{ f \in \bar{A} \mid \Psi'_{PQ} f(x) - f(x) \xrightarrow{\text{norm}} 0, \quad x \to 0 \}$ *where*

$$(5.81) \qquad \Psi_{PQ} f(x) = V_x \begin{pmatrix} P_x f_1 P_x & P_x f_1 Q_x U_x^* \\ U_x Q_x f_1 P_x & Q_{-x} f_2 Q_{-x} \end{pmatrix} V_x^{-1} \in M_2(\mathcal{K}(L^2(\mathbb{R}))$$

for f *with* $f(x) \xrightarrow{*\text{-st}} \begin{pmatrix} f_1 & 0 \\ 0 & f_2 \end{pmatrix}, \quad x \to 0.$

If we replace Ψ'_{PQ} *by* Ψ''_{PQ} *where*

$$\Psi''_{PQ} f(x) = V_x \begin{pmatrix} \sim & U_x^* P_{-x} f_2 Q_{-x} \\ \sim & \sim \end{pmatrix} V_x^{-1}$$

then the assertion is still true.

Now we are at the position to prove the main theorems of this paper. We come back to the (p+q)-dimensional case.

THEOREM 5.23. *There is a natural imbedding* Ψ *mapping the* C^**-algebra* $C^*(G(p,q))$ *into the (non-separable)* C^**-algebra*

$$\mathcal{C} = C^b(S^{p-1}\times S^{q-1}\times(0,\infty),\ M_2(\mathcal{K}(L^2(\mathbb{R})))) \quad . \tag{5.82}$$

Let the image of Ψ *be* $\mathcal{A}$, *then for every* $f\in\mathcal{A}$ *we have*

i) $f(m) \xrightarrow{\text{norm}} 0$ *when* $m=(x,y,t)\to\infty$.

ii) *For any* $x\in S^{p-1}$, $y\in S^{q-1}$, $m\in S^{p-1}\times S^{q-1}\times(0,\infty)$, *when* $m\to(x,y,0)$, *then*

$$f(m) \xrightarrow{*\text{-st}} \begin{pmatrix} f_1(y) & 0 \\ 0 & f_2(x) \end{pmatrix} \tag{5.83}$$

where $(f_1(y), f_2(x)) \in C^*((S^*-I)\oplus 0)\oplus C^*(0\oplus(S-I))$ *such that* $\pi(f_1(y)) = \overline{\pi(f_2(x))}$ *(for any* $x\in S^{p-1}$, $y\in S^{q-1}$*)*

iii) *In addition to* (5.83),

$$\|f(m)\| \longrightarrow \left\|\begin{pmatrix} f_1(y) & 0 \\ 0 & f_2(x) \end{pmatrix}\right\|$$

as $m\to(x,y,0)$.

Furthermore, we have the following exact sequences (see (2.8), (2.9), (2.10), (2.22) *and Theorem 5.10).*

$$\begin{array}{ccccccccc} 0 & \longrightarrow & C_0(U_1)\rtimes\mathbb{R} & \longrightarrow & C^*(G(p,q))^+ & \longrightarrow & B^+ & \longrightarrow & 0 \\ & & \downarrow\simeq & & \simeq\downarrow\Psi & & \downarrow\simeq & & \\ 0 & \longrightarrow & A_{U_1} & \longrightarrow & \mathcal{A}^+ & \longrightarrow & \bar{B} & \longrightarrow & 0 \end{array} \tag{5.84}$$

<u>Proof</u>. For any $(x,y)\in S^{p-1}\times S^{q-1}$, we have an embedding Ψ_{PQ} from $C_0(\dot{S}_{xy})\rtimes\mathbb{R}$ into $\bar{C}$ (see (5.80)). Let $g\in C^*(G(p,q))$. We define $\Psi(g) = \mathrm{Ad}_V\cdot\hat{\psi}(g)$. The construction of an embedding $\hat{\psi}$ of

$C^*(G(p,q))$ is the same as that given in the proof of Corollary 5.8.

$$\begin{array}{ccccc} (x,y,t) & \overset{\hat{\psi}}{\longmapsto} & (\hat{\psi}_{xy}(g))(t) & \in & \mathcal{K}(P_t L^2(\mathbb{R}) \oplus Q_{-t} L^2(\mathbb{R})) \\ & \searrow^{\Psi(g)} & \downarrow & & \cong \downarrow Ad_{V_t} \\ & & (\Psi_{xy}(g))(t) & \in & \mathcal{K}(L^2(\mathbb{R}) \oplus L^2(\mathbb{R})) \end{array}$$

We first need to show that $\Psi(g)$ is norm continuous on $S^{p-1} \times S^{q-1} \times (0,\infty)$. By Corollary 5.8, this is true for $g \in C_0(U) \rtimes \mathbb{R} \subset C^*(G(p,q))$, since the proof was based on Lemma 3.1 where the norm continuity on $S^{p-1} \times S^{q-1} \times (0,\infty)$ is true not only for $C_0(U) \rtimes \mathbb{R}$ but also for $C^*(G(p,q))$ as well. So the same reasoning shows $\hat{\psi}(g)$ is norm continuous for $g \in C^*(G(p,q))$. It follows that $\Psi(g) = Ad_V \circ \hat{\psi}(g)$ is also norm continuous (see (5.57).

From Corollary 3.2 and the definition of $\hat{\psi}$ (see (5.44)) we have $\hat{\psi}g(m) \to 0$ as $m \to \infty$. Thus $\Psi g(m) \to 0$ as $m \to \infty$. This proves (i).

For (ii), Lemma 5.1 tells us that given any $g \in C^*(G(p,q))$, fix $(x,y) \in S^{p-1} \times S^{q-1}$ and denote the restriction of g on the quarter plane (which is identified with the half plane model) still by g. Then

$$\psi(g)(x,y,t) = \hat{\psi}_{xy}(g)(t) \longrightarrow \begin{pmatrix} \pi_y(g) & 0 \\ 0 & \pi_x(g) \end{pmatrix}$$

According to the proof of Theorem 2.5 we have

$$(\pi_y(g), \pi_x(g)) \in C^*((S^*-I) \oplus 0) \oplus C^*(0 \oplus (S-I))$$

with $\pi(\pi_y(g) = \pi(\pi_x(g)) \in C(S^1)$ depending only on g.

Now let's change the assumption $(x,y,t) \to (x,y,0)$ by

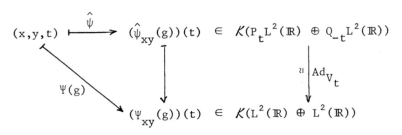

$m \in S^{p-1} \times S^{q-1} \times (0,\infty)$, $m \to (x,y,0)$. Consider the estimate for (5.17). Here we let g be defined on $\mathbb{R}^{p+q+1}$, and replace N_x in (5.17) by $N_t^{(x,y)}$, N_+ by $N_+^{(x,y)}$. We may still assume $g \in C_c(\mathbb{R}, C_c(\mathbb{R}^{p+q}))$. The same discussion is still valid.

The same observation applies for (5.20). So (ii) holds for $\hat{\psi}g$, $g \in C^*(G(p,q))$ and thus it holds for any $f \in \mathcal{A}$, $f = \mathrm{Ad}_V\hat{\psi}(g)$.

Furthermore, the preceding observation also applies to Lemma 5.15 so $\|\hat{\psi}(g)(m)\| \longrightarrow \left\|\begin{pmatrix} f_1(y) & 0 \\ 0 & f_2(x)\end{pmatrix}\right\|$ when $m \to (x,y,0)$. Notice that $\{V_x\}$, $\{V_x^{-1}\}$ are isometries, thus (iii) holds for any $f = \mathrm{Ad}_V\hat{\psi}(g)$.

Next we claim that Ψ is injective. The proof is identical to that in the proof of Corollary 5.8. We do not repeat it.

The exact sequence (5.84) is clear. For the mapping involving B, see (2.39) and (2.40). Q.E.D.

Corresponding to Theorem 5.21' we have the second characterization of $C^*(G(p,q))$ which pins down the C^*-algebra $\mathcal{A}$ (Theorem 5.23) among other C*-subalgebras of $\mathcal{C}$ which also satisfies the conditions (i), (ii) and (iii) in Theorem 5.23.

THEOREM 5.24. *The natural embedding* Ψ *mapping* $C^*(G(p,q))$ *onto the* C*-*subalgebra* $\mathcal{A}$ *of* $\mathcal{C}$ *generated by the ideal* A_U *(see Corollary 5.8 and* (4.18)*) with one more generator.*

$$\Psi' g_0 : (x,y,t) \longmapsto V_t \hat{\psi}'_{xy}(g_0)(t)V_t^{-1}$$

(see (5.75)*). We have the following exact sequence (see* (2.4)*):*

$$
(5.85)\qquad
\begin{array}{ccccccccc}
0 & \longrightarrow & C_0(U)\rtimes \mathbb{R} & \longrightarrow & C^*(G(p,q)) & \longrightarrow & C_0(\mathbb{R}) & \longrightarrow & 0\\
 & & \wr\big\downarrow \Psi & & \wr\big\downarrow \Psi & & \Big\| & & \\
0 & \longrightarrow & A_U & \longrightarrow & \mathcal{A} & \longrightarrow & C_0(\mathbb{R}) & \longrightarrow & 0\\
 & & & & \Psi' g_0 & \longrightarrow & \theta - 1 & &
\end{array}
$$

So a dense subalgebra of $C^*(G(p,q))$ is given by Lemma 5.11 with $I = A_U$ and $T = \Psi' g_0$. Q.E.D.

Finally, corresponding to Theorem 5.22', we have the third characterization of $C^*(G(p,q))$.

THEOREM 5.25. *Let* $\bar{\mathcal{A}}$ *be the (non-separable)* C^**-algebra:*

$$
\bar{\mathcal{A}} = \Big\{ f \in C^b(S^{p-1}\times S^{q-1}\times(0,\infty),\ M_2(\mathcal{K}(L^2(\mathbb{R})))) \text{ such that}
$$

i) $f(m) \xrightarrow{\text{norm}} 0$ *as* $m \to \infty$

ii) $f(m) \xrightarrow{*\text{-st}} \begin{pmatrix} f_1(y) & 0 \\ 0 & f_2(x) \end{pmatrix}$ *as* $m \to (x,y,0)$ *where*

$f_1 \in C(S^{q-1}, C^*((S^*-I)\oplus 0)$ *and* $f_2 \in C(S^{p-1}, C^*(0\oplus(S-I))$

satisfying $\pi(f_1(y)) = \pi(f_2(x))$ *for* $(x,y)\in S^{p-1}\times S^{q-1}\Big\}$.

Then the natural isomorphism Ψ *maps* $C^*(G(p,q))$ *onto the* C^**-subalgebra* $\mathcal{A}$ *of* $\bar{\mathcal{A}}$ *given by*

$$
\mathcal{A} = \{ f\in\bar{\mathcal{A}} \mid \Psi' f(m) - f(m) \xrightarrow{\text{norm}} 0 \text{ when } t(m)\to 0\} \quad \begin{pmatrix} m = (x,y,t) \\ \text{then } t(m) = t \end{pmatrix}
$$

where

$$
(5.86)\qquad \Psi' f(x,y,t) = V_t \begin{pmatrix} P_t f_1(y) P_t & P_t f_1(y) Q_t U_t^* \\ U_t^* Q_t f_1(y) P_t & Q_{-t} f_2(x) Q_{-t} \end{pmatrix} V_t^{-1} \in M_2(\mathcal{K}(L^2(\mathbb{R})))
$$

for $f\in\bar{\mathcal{A}}$ *with* $f(x,y,t) \xrightarrow{*\text{-st}} \begin{pmatrix} f_1(y) & 0 \\ 0 & f_2(x) \end{pmatrix}$, $\quad t\to 0$.

The preceding assertion is still true if we replace Ψ' by Ψ'', where

$$(5.87)\qquad \Psi'' f(x,y,t) = V_t \begin{pmatrix} \sim & U_t^* P_{-t} f_2(x) Q_{-t} \\ \sim & \sim \end{pmatrix} V_t^{-1} .$$

Notation: for projections $\{P_t\},\{Q_t\}_{t\geq 0}$ and unitaries $\{U_t\}$, see the beginning of §5. For partial isometries V_t, V_t^-, see Lemma 5.4.

COROLLARY 5.26. *The natural isomorphism* Ψ *identifies* $C^*(G(p,q))$ *with the* C^**-subalgebra* $\mathcal{A}$ *of* $\bar{\mathcal{A}}$ *(Theorem 5.25), where* $\mathcal{A}$ *consists exactly of the elements* f *of* $\bar{\mathcal{A}}$ *of the following form:*

$$f = f_0 + f'$$

where $f_0 \in C_0(S^{p-1} \times S^{q-1} \times (0,\infty), M_2(\mathcal{K}))$

and $f'\colon S^{p-1} \times S^{q-1} \times (0,\infty) \longrightarrow M_2(\mathcal{K})$

is given by (5.56); $f' = \Psi' f$. *Equivalently*

$$f = \tilde{f}_0 + f''$$

where $\tilde{f}_0 \in C_0(S^{p-1} \times S^{q-1} \times (0,\infty), M_2(\mathcal{K}))$

and $f'' = \Psi'' f$

is given by (5.57) *(see Lemma 5.16).*

References

[Ake] C. A. Akemann, G. K. Pedersen and J. Tomiyama, "Multipliers of C^*-algebras," J. Functional Analysis 13 (1973), 277-301.

[A-K] L. Auslander and B. Kostant, "Quantization and representations of solvable Lie groups," Bull. A.M.S. 73, 692-695 (1967).

[Ar 1] W. B. Arveson, In invitation to C^*-algebras, Grad. Text. Math. Vol.39, Springer-Verlager 19.

[Ar 2] W. B. Arveson, "Notes on extensions of C^*-algebras," Duke Math. J. 44 (1977), 329-355.

[Bl] B. Blackadar , "K-theory and Operator Algebras," MSRI Series, Springer-Verlag, 1986.

[B-M] R. Boyer and R. Martin, "The group C^*-algebra of the DeSitter group,"

[B-D-F] L. G. Brown, R. G. Douglas and P. A. Fillmore, "Extensions of C^*-algebras and K-homology," Ann. of Math. 105 (1977), 265-324.

[Bus] R. C. Busby, "Double centralizers and extensions of C^*-algebras," Trans. Amer. Math. Soc. 132 (1968(, 79-99.

[C-E] M.-D. Choi and E. G. Effors, "The completely positive lifting problem for C^*-algebras," Ann. of Math. (2) 104 (1976), 585-609.

[C-M] A. Connes and H. Moskowici, "The L^2-index theorem for homogeneous spaces of Lie groups," Ann. Math. 115 (1982), 291-330.

[Con 1] A. Connes, "An analogue of the Thom isomorphism for crossed products of a C^*-algebra by an action of $\mathbb{R}$," Advances in Math. 39 (1981), 31-35.

[Con 2] A. Connes, "A survey of foliations and operator algebras," Proceedings of Symp. in Pure Math. 38 (1982), part 1.

[Con 3] A. Connes, "Sur la theorie non commutative de l'integation," Lecture Notes in Math. 725 (Springer, 1979), pp. 19-143.

[Del] C. Delaroche, "Extensions des C^*-algebras," Bull. Soc. Math. France, Memoire 29 (1972).

[Dix] J. Dixmier, C^*-Algebras, vol. 15 (North-Holland, Mathematical Library, 1977).

[D] R. Douglas, C^*-algebra Extensions and K-Homology, Ann. Math. Stud., (Princeton Press, 1980).

[Eff] E. G. Effros, "Aspects of Non-commutative Geometry," in Algèbres d'opérateurs et leur applications en physique mathématique, Marseille, 1977, Colloques internationaux du C.N.R.S. No. 274.

[EH] E. G. Effros and F. Hahn, "Locally compact transformation groups and C^*-algebras," Mem. Amer. Math. Soc. 75 (1967).

[EV] B. Evans, C^*-bundles and compact transformation groups," Memoirs of A.M.S. no. 269 (1982).

[Fell] J. M. G. Fell, "The structure of algebras of operator fields," Acta Math. 106 (1961), 233-280.

[F-M] A. T. Fomenko and A. S. Miščenko, "An index theorem for C^*-algebra Izvestia, A.P. U.S.S.R., 43 (1979), 831-859 [Russian].

[Gor] N. V. Gorbachef, "The C^*-algebra of Heisenberg group" [Russian], Uspek. Mat. Nauk. 35, no. 6 (1980), 157-158.

[Gr] P. Green, "C^*-algebras of transformation groups with smooth orbit space," Pacific Jour. of Math. 72, no. 1 (1977).

[Kad] R. V. Kadison and J. R. Ringrose, Fundamentals of the Theory of Operator Algebras, I, II, Acad. Press, 1985.

[Kas 1] G. G. Kasparov, "The K-Functor in the theory of extensions of C^*-algebras," Funk. Anal. i Prilozen 13, no. 4 (1979), 73-74; [Func. Anal. Appl. 13 (1979), 296-297).

[Kas 2] G. G. Kasparov, "Operator K-functions and extensions of C^*-algebras," Izvestija Akademii Nauk SSSR Ser. Math. 44, no. 3 (1980), 511-636.

[Kir] A. A. Kirillov, Elements of Group Representation Theory, Springer-Verlag.

[K-M] H. Kraljevic and D. Milicic, "The C^*-algebra of the universal covering group of $SL(2,\mathbb{R})$," Glasnik Mat. Ser. III, 7 (1972), 35-48.

[L1] R. Y. Lee, "On the C^*-algebras of operator fields," Indiana Univ. Math. J. 25, no. 4 (1976), 303-314.

[L2] R. Y. Lee, "Full algebras of operator fields trivial except at one point," Indiana Univ. Math. J. 26 (1977), 351-372.

[Mac] S. MacLane, Homology, Springer-Verlage (1963).

[M-S] C. C. Moore and C. Schochet, "Analysis on Foliated Spaces," MSRI Series, Springer-Verlag, to appear.

[Mil] D. Milicic, "Topological representations of the group C^*-algebra of $SL(2,\mathbb{R})$," Glasnik Mat. Ser. III, 6 (1971), 231-246.

[M-R] C. C. Moore and J. Rosenberg, "Groups with T_1-primitive ideal spaces," J. Func. Anal. 22 (1976), 204-224.

[Ped] G. Pedersen, C^*-algebras and Their Automorphism Groups, (Academic Press, New York, 1979).

[Per] F. Perdrizet, "Topologie et traces sur les C^*-algebras," Bull. Soc. Math. France 99 (1971), 193-239.

[P-P-V] M. Pimsner, S. Popa and D. Voiculescu, "Homogeneous C^*-extensions of $C(X) \otimes K(H)$, I," J. Operator Theory 1 (1979), 55-108; II, ibid.

[Pog] D. Pogunkte, "Simple quotients of group C^*-algebras for two step nilpotent groups and connected Lie groups," Math. Anne.

[Puk] L. Pukansky, "Unitary representation of Lie groups and generalized symplectic geometry," Proc. Sympos. Pure Math. 38, Amer. Math. Soc. (1982), 435-466.

[Ren] J. Renault, "A groupoid approach to C^*-algebras," Lecture Notes in Math 793, (Springer-Verlag, 1976).

[Rie 1] M. A. Rieffel, "C^*-algebras associated with irrational rotations," Pac. J. Math. 93 (1981), 415-429.

[Rie 2] M. A. Rieffel, "Projective modules over higher dimensional non-commutative tori," preprint.

[R1] J. Rosenberg, "The C^*-algebras of some real and p-adic solvable groups," Pacific Jour. of Math. 65, no. 1 (1976).

[R2] J. Rosenberg, "Homological invariants of extensions of C^*-algebras," Proc. of Sym. in Pure Math. 38 (1982), part 1.

[RS] J. Rosenberg and C. Schochet, "Comparing functors classifying extensions of C^*-algebras," Jour. Operator Theory 5 (1981), 267-282

[R-S 2] J. Rosenberg and C. Schochet, "The Künneth theorem and the universal coefficient theorem for equivariant K-theory and KK-theory," Memoirs AMS, Vol. 348, 1986.

[S-V] V. M. Son and H. H. Viet, "Sur la structure des C^*-algebras d'une classe de groupes de Lie," Jour. Operator Theory 11 (1984), 77-90.

[Tak] M. Takasaki, Theory of Operator Algebras I, Springer-Verlag, 1979, II to appear.

[Tay] J. L. Taylor, "Banach algebras and topology," in Algebras in Analysis, J. H. Williamson, ed., (Academic Press, London-New York, 1975), pp. 118-186.

[Tor] A. M. Torpe, "K-theory for the leaf space of foliations by Reeb components," Ph.D. thesis.

[Val] A. Valette, "K-theory for the reduced C^*-algebra of semi-simple Lie group with real rank one," Quarterly J. of Math., Oxford, Série 2, 35 (1984), 334-359.

[Viet] H. H. Viet, "Sur la structure des C^*-algebres d'une classe de groupes de Lie résolubles de dimension 3," to appear in Acta Math. Vietnam (1985).

[Vo] D. Voiculescu, "Remarks on the singular extension in the C^*-algebra of the Heisenberg group," J. Oper. Theory 5 (1981), 147-170.

[Was] A. Wasserman, "Une démonstration de la conjecture de Connes-Kasparov pour les groupes de Lie linéares conveses réductifs,"

[W1] X. Wang, "On the C^*-algebras of Foliations of the Plane," Lec. Notes of Math. Vol. 1257, Springer-Verlag, (1987).

[W2] X. Wang, "Non-commutative CW complexes," Contemp. Math. A.M.S. 70 (1988), 303-322; edited by J. Kaminker and C. Schochet.

[W3] X. Wang, "Les C^*-algèbres d'une classe de groupes de Lie résolubles," C. R. Acad. Sci. Paris t.306 (1988), 765-767.

[W4] X. Wang and M. Hirsch, "Foliations of planar regions and CCR C^*-algebras with infinite composition length," Amer. J. of Math. 109 (1987), 797-806.

[W5] X. Wang, "On the relation between C*-algebras of foliations and those of their coverings," Proc. of Amer.. Math. Soc. 102 (1988), 355-360.

[W6] X. Wang, "C*-algebras of Morse-Smale flows on two-manifolds," (1986), to appear in Ergodic Theory and Dynamical Systems.

[Wil] D. Williams, "The topology of the primitive ideal space of transformation group C*-algebras and CCR transformation group C*-algebras," Trans. A.M.S. 266, no. 2 (1981).

[Zek] R. Zekri, "A new description of Kasparov's theory of C^*-algebra extensions," Preprint, Centre de Physique Théorique, CNRS, (1987).

[Zep] D. N. Z'ep, "Structure of the group C^*-algebra of the group of affine transformations of a straight line," Funct. Anal. Appl. 9 (1975), 58-60.

Notation

Reader's Guide*

The first chapter, which is devoted to some generalities about transfo mation group C^*-algebras and foliations, makes the paper accessible to non specialists.

In chapter 2, the author gives several descriptions of the group C^*-algebra $C^*(G(p,q))^+$ by means of exact sequences. He first gives a complete description of $C^*(G(0,m))^+$ as a subalgebra of $C(\mathbf{S}^{m-1}, C^*(S))$, where $C^*(S)$ is the C^*-algebra of the shift. Then, he proves the existence of a short exact sequence

$$0 \rightarrow C^*(U,F) \rightarrow C^*(G(p,q))^+ \rightarrow C(\mathbf{S}^1) \rightarrow 0$$

the foliation algebra $C^*(U,F)$ being again described by an exact sequence

$$0 \rightarrow C_0(\mathbf{S}^{p-1}\times\mathbf{S}^{q-1}\times(0,+\infty)) \otimes \mathbf{K} \rightarrow C^*(U,F) \rightarrow C(\mathbf{S}^{p-1}\cup\mathbf{S}^{q-1}, \mathbf{K}) \rightarrow 0$$

where $\mathbf{K}$ denotes the algebra of all compact operators in $L^2(\mathbf{R})$. On the other hand, the author gives another description of $C^*(G(p,q))^+$ by a cross of short exact sequences

$$\begin{array}{ccccccc}
 & & & & 0 & & \\
 & & & & \uparrow & & \\
 & & & & C(S^1) & & \\
 & & & & \uparrow & & \\
0 \rightarrow & C_0(\mathbf{S}^{p-1}\times\mathbf{S}^{q-1}\times(0,+\infty)) \otimes \mathbf{K} & \rightarrow & C^*(G(p,q))^+ & \rightarrow B^+ & \rightarrow & 0 \\
 & & & & \uparrow & & \\
 & & & & C(\mathbf{S}^{p-1}\cup\mathbf{S}^{q-1}, \mathbf{K}) & & \\
 & & & & \uparrow & & \\
 & & & & 0 & &
\end{array}$$

The connecting maps in the six-term exact sequence in K-theory correspondin to the vertical exact sequence are computed. Finally, the algebra B^+ is described as a subalgebra of $C(\mathbf{S}^{p-1}\cup\mathbf{S}^{q-1}, C^*(S))$, using techniques due to Green and Rosenberg. As a corollary, the author obtains a result previousl obtained by Z'ep on the structure of the C^*-algebra of the "ax+b" group.

In chapter 3, the author shows how to write $C^*(G(p,q))^+$ as a continuous field of C^*-algebras over some dense open subset of the spectrum, homeomorphic to $\mathbf{S}^{p-1}\times\mathbf{S}^{q-1}\times(0,+\infty)$. More precisely, $C^*(G,p,q))^+$ is embedded as a

---

*We would like to express our appreciation to the referee of this paper for supplying this Guide for the reader.

subalgebra in $C^b(\mathbf{S}^{p-1}\times\mathbf{S}^{q-1}\times(0,+\infty),\ \mathbf{K}(L^2(\mathbf{R})))$, the C*-algebra of all bounded functions on $\mathbf{S}^{p-1}\times\mathbf{S}^{q-1}\times(0,+\infty)$, with compact operator values. In addition, the boundary values of the functions in the image of $C^*(G(p,q))^+$ are computed. Finally, the image of any $g \in C^*(G(p,q))^+$ via the map π of the exact sequence

$$0 \to C^*(U,F) \to C^*(G(p,q))^+ \xrightarrow{\pi} C(\mathbf{S}^1) \approx C_0(\mathbf{R})^+ \to 0$$

is identified.

Chapter 4 is devoted to a complete description of the foliation algebra $C^*(U,F)$. † This algebra is first described as a subalgebra of $C_0(\mathbf{S}^{p-1}\times\mathbf{S}^{q-1}\times[0,1),\ M_2(\mathbf{K}))$. This allows us to compute in an original way the connecting maps of the six-term exact sequence in K-theory associated with the exact sequence

$$0 \to C_0(\mathbf{S}^{p-1}\times\mathbf{S}^{q-1}\times(0,+\infty)) \otimes \mathbf{K} \to C^*(U,F) \to C(\mathbf{S}^{p-1}\cup\mathbf{S}^{q-1},\ \mathbf{K}) \to 0$$

Particular attention is called to the case $p = q = 1$, where the situation is reminiscent to that in the work of A. M. Torpe about Reeb's foliation. However, the methods used in the characterization of C*-algebras are totally different. Finally, the author computes the connecting maps of the 6-term exact sequence in K-theory associated with the "deunitalization" of the exact sequence

$$0 \to C_0(\mathbf{S}^{p-1}\times\mathbf{S}^{q-1}\times(0,+\infty)) \otimes \mathbf{K} \to C^*(G(p,q))^+ \to B^+ \to 0$$

The last chapter gives a complete description of $C^*(G(p,q))$ as a subalgebra of $C^b(\mathbf{S}^{p-1}\times\mathbf{S}^{q-1}\times[0,\infty,\ M_2[\mathbf{K}(L^2(\mathbf{R}))])$. The main structure theorem is based on the description of an explicit isomorphism from $C\ (U)\times\mathbf{R}$, the natural ideal of $C^*(G(p,q))^+$ onto $C^*(U,F)$, which has already been described as a subalgebra of $C\ (\mathbf{S}^{p-1}\times\mathbf{S}^{q-1}\times[0,\infty), M_2(\mathbf{K}))$. In fact, two descriptions of $C^*(G(p,q))$ are given, corresponding to the short exact sequences

$$0 \to C_0(\mathbf{S}^{p-1}\times\mathbf{S}^{q-1}\times(0,+\infty)) \otimes \mathbf{K} \to C^*(G(p,q))^+ \to B^+ \to 0$$

and

$$0 \to C^*(U,F) \to C^*(G,p,q))^+ \to C(\mathbf{S}^1) \to 0$$

†They are of fundamental importance in the structure of C*-algebras of Morse-Smale flows in any manifolds; see [W6].